START A
COMMUNITY
FOOD
GARDEN

START A COMMUNITY FOOD GARDEN

The Essential Handbook

LaMANDA JOY

TIMBER PRESS
Portland + London

" I'M A BIG BELIEVER IN COMMUNITY GARDENS, BOTH BECAUSE OF THEIR BEAUTY AND FOR THEIR ACCESS TO PROVIDING FRESH FRUITS AND VEGETABLES TO SO MANY COMMUNITIES ACROSS THIS NATION AND THE WORLD. **"**

—FIRST LADY MICHELLE OBAMA

Remarks to U.S. Department of Agriculture, February 19, 2009

CONTENTS

Preface   Lot Lust, Rosie the Riveter, and Corporate Burnout—or Why I Became a Community Gardener   **6**

Introduction   So You Want to Start a Community Garden?   **10**

PART ONE | Gathering Your Community

1. **Without Community, It's Just a Garden: Getting Organized**   **17**

➡ **Six Successful Community Gardens: Case Studies**   **21**

2. **Get the Party Started: Meetings with a Mission**   **35**

PART TWO | Support Structures

3. **Bringing the Garden to Life: Planning and Design**   **59**

4. **Taking Care of Garden Business: A Structure for Sustainability**   **85**

PART THREE | Managing the Community and the Garden

5. **Mobilizing: Developing a Team of Gardeners and Volunteers**   **103**

6. **The Year-Round Community: Keeping It Fun**   **117**

7. **Groundwork for Success: Teaching New Gardeners**   **129**

8. **Twenty-One Vegetables to Sow, Harvest, Store, and Serve**   **169**

Resources and Books   **186**

Metric Conversions   **191**

Acknowledgments   **192**

Index   **194**

PREFACE

Lot Lust, Rosie the Riveter, and Corporate Burnout—or Why I Became a Community Gardener

Community activism, in the form of community gardening or any activity, wasn't something I had planned for my life. After studying musical theater in college I ended up, curiously, in the marketing world and, for almost twenty years, worked my way up from being a project manager in boutique marketing agencies to being an executive at a large event company. My teams within all these jobs were creatives—designers, producers, directors. I loved how creative-team ingenuity could come up with incredible solutions to our clients' marketing and communication dilemmas. But as I climbed the corporate ladder, traveled more, and had less time for my friends and family, I began to realize that something was missing. I longed for a greater connection with others and a more grounded lifestyle.

Food growing had always been my happy place. My father taught me to garden while I was growing up in rural Oregon. Many years later, as an urbanite in Chicago, I realized that this food-growing ability meant a lot to me—as a way to have the best produce, but also as an escape from my increasingly challenging career. After seven springs, suffering miserably as a gardenless gardener living in a condo, my husband, Peter, woke up one late-winter morning and said, "Should we go look for a house? Wait. Should we go look for a yard?" And so we did, and we found our yard, with a house attached to it.

Our yarden, as I liked to call it, quickly transformed from 3,500 square feet of lawn and little else into an organic, heirloom garden paradise. I was so excited to be able to grow food again, I wanted to share my experiences and connect with other food gardeners in Chicago. So I started a blog called *The Yarden* to reach out to other like-minded people. Sadly, I found that there weren't many who knew how to grow their own food. Lots of people were interested—even desperate—to learn this skill, but few were practitioners.

Around this time we were exploring our new neighborhood and my lot lust (when you see an empty lot and want to turn it into a garden) flared up. Living on the congested North Side of Chicago, there weren't a lot of empty lots to lust after, so I fixated on one very close to my house at Peterson and Campbell Avenues.

A little relevant background: both of my parents were actively involved in World War II. My mother was a Rosie the Riveter and my father was with the Allied occupation forces in Japan. Like many people of their generation who had lived through both the Great Depression and World War II, my parents were very self-sufficient, pull-yourself-up-by-your-bootstraps kind of people. I was inspired by them, and much of that ethos rubbed off on me. However, the over-developed sense of responsibility I credit to (and sometimes blame on) my parents, was burning me out at work. I had become tired of using my talents to make money for companies whose values I didn't share. I was looking for a way to contribute in a meaningful way to my community. You could call it midlife crisis, I suppose. But instead of buying a very expensive car or getting a divorce, I started a community garden.

Back to that empty lot. While shopping at Muller Meats, our local butcher shop, I noticed a photo on the wall of a World War II victory garden. I asked the proprietors, Ruben and Irv, about the photo, and they explained that it was a large garden on Peterson Avenue during the war. I was familiar with the concept of victory gardens—how people on the home front had been forced to augment their families' food needs. But seeing that photo, on that day, as a hungry gardener-transplant—well, I got very curious. In Oregon, many people know how to grow their own food; this agricultural know-how is part of the state's heritage, and was still strong when I was growing up. I wondered if it was the same in Chicago in the 1940s. Did those city dwellers have a cultural history that predisposed them to know how to grow their own food during the war?

They say curiosity killed the cat. In my case, it was obsession that almost did me in. I became engrossed in the story of how Chicago fed itself during the Second World War. Much to my surprise, I learned that 90 percent of the people who grew food then in Chicago had never gardened before. They weren't landscape gardeners who changed their tune and tried growing vegetables. They were flat-out garden rookies. And there were lots of them: Chicago led the nation in victory gardens during the war, with 1,500 community gardens and more than 250,000 home gardens. The largest victory garden in the United States was in Chicago.

The city was able to teach its citizens how to garden through a concerted educational effort, utilizing newspaper and radio, live demonstration gardens, classes, and an organized system of block captains, who were citywide garden leaders. This juggernaut of information and support created an atmosphere in which community gardens thrived, tens of thousands of home gardens sprouted up, and, some say, more than 50 percent of the produce consumed in the city during the war was homegrown.

Fast forward to 2010—to me and my yarden, my "if you don't like something, do something about it" upbringing, that empty lot on Peterson and Campbell, and that photo on the butcher shop wall—it all came together in one explosion of ideas and excitement on a spring day in 2010 as I drove by that empty lot once more, and realized it was the site of one of the victory gardens in the photo at the butcher shop.

I got an idea: What if I recreated a food garden almost 70 years later on that same spot? I could follow the model that was used during the war—revive the victory garden concept and teach people how to grow their own food. I talked with our alderman (a local government representative in Chicago) who got permission for the land from the owners, a local nonprofit. I started reaching out to neighbors and local businesses. I thought it would be great if twenty people wanted to garden together. As I was taking these fledgling steps with community leaders, nonprofits, and neighbors, little did I know that Peterson Garden Project would become the largest organic, edible garden in the city. Nor did I know that four years later it would encompass nine gardens, 4,000-plus gardeners and volunteers, a full-blown education program, and a home cooking school—and that it would completely alter the course of my life.

I tell you all this because you, too, may be ready to take the plunge into becoming a community garden leader. Your journey may not be as life-altering as mine was, but I promise that your experience with the community garden process will change you—most likely, for the better.

The idea for this book came about because I'm asked a lot about how to start a community garden. Usually the focus is where to get the lumber or how to secure land, but, as you'll learn while reading this book, a community garden is much more than the building materials. A community garden is an exercise in humanity, transformation, and joy.

It is my sincere wish that your community garden thrive, that you learn from the mistakes that I and other community garden leaders have made—and from the best practices those missteps have fostered. I also hope that your good work, wherever you are on this planet of ours, changes empty lots and empty lives into something remarkable: the beautiful place I like to call community.

INTRODUCTION   *So You Want to Start a Community Garden?*

You've been eyeing that weedy, empty lot at the end of the block. Or the back parcel that used to be lawn at your house of worship. Maybe your employer is considering installing a community garden to fulfill its social mission, or the company wants a workplace garden on their corporate campus. Or maybe you have an extra big suburban lot you'd like to share with neighbors.

You are not alone. The idea of a community garden is percolating in a lot of brains worldwide these days. According to recent research studies from Rutgers University, transformation of vacant land into verdant growing places is increasingly perceived as a benefit to the communities these gardens serve. More and more of this type of land use is being recognized as legitimate and sustainable by city and local governments, reducing the barriers to starting and maintaining gardens on public land.

Communities with food gardens as permanent fixtures acknowledge the positive effect on the lives of low-income, minority, and immigrant or refugee populations, as well as seniors, children, and the general public. Essentially, community gardens benefit everyone. And ongoing research shows that these benefits are multifaceted, enhancing—through positive social interactions and accessibility to healthy fresh food—the fabric of our towns, cities, and, increasingly, rural areas. Grassroots gardening as a movement continues to grow as a meaningful part of everyday life and is creeping into the mainstream experience.

DO SOME HOMEWORK

After that ringing endorsement, what I'm about to say may be the last thing you'd expect. But the truth is, *starting* a community garden may not be the only—or even the best—solution for your circumstances. Starting anything from the ground up is hard work, and requires long-term dedication. Before you make that commitment, ask around to see if there are other community gardens nearby. If there are, observe them to determine if they already meet the needs of you and your group. Does your organization have something to offer that this garden needs? Is the whole better than the sum of the parts?

Even if you are determined to create your own community garden, spending a season working with other garden leaders will likely give you invaluable hands-on experience, and ultimately help your new garden's chances of long-term survival.

But let's say there's not a community garden for miles around. Lots of interest means lots of good ideas. And lots of good ideas means lots of people who are invested in the success of the potential garden. This is a good thing.

URBAN AG VS. COMMUNITY GARDENS: EXACTLY THE SAME BUT DIFFERENT

What type of project are you doing? It's a food garden, of course! That's easy—well, maybe not. There are a lot of terms used for food gardening projects these days. Sometimes they're used interchangeably and yet mean very different things. Here's a quick breakdown.

Urban farms are a lot like general agriculture, just on a smaller scale. These farms are all about volume production growing for consumer sale in a city or suburban environment. There is an economic and sometimes a job-creation component to these projects, and gardening techniques are geared for mass production. Urban farms are generally zoned differently, and regulations are more stringent than for a community garden, because of the business component and the safety requirements of selling food to the public.

Community food gardens are built to serve a group of people living in close proximity, who share a common goal. Generally, the food is not sold and is grown for the gardeners' use or distributed to neighborhood food and nutrition agencies. The community members collectively do the work of tending the garden. If the community garden is part of a larger organization, there may or may not be paid staff to help administer the garden. Oftentimes, community gardens are run 100 percent by volunteers.

Workplace gardens are similar to community gardens, except the community is pre-defined by the company sponsoring or supporting the garden. Institutions such as museums and hospitals often have workplace gardens that provide a positive outlet for their employees, but may have additional benefits such as an outdoor exhibit (in the case of a museum), or a hands-on learning space about topics such as nutrition (in the case of a hospital). Increasingly, larger businesses are designating part of their corporate campuses for employee gardens.

School gardens may be similar to community gardens in that the food is not sold and the garden is part of a community within the school. However, school gardens are often created and used as a form of curriculum for the students. Another unique aspect of school gardens is that school is generally out during the summer, so sustainability plans are needed to keep the garden going through the non-school months. The students who started the garden in spring are not necessarily the ones tending the garden during the main growing season of summer, or even in the fall, when school starts again. Sometimes community members help with these efforts.

Then there are community gardens that call themselves urban farms and have small farmers' markets where each individual gardener contributes a portion of what they grow to the greater good. And, urban farms run by volunteers who provide community garden space in exchange for fieldwork to grow produce that is sold. And, school gardens where the produce grown is sold to the school for use in the cafeteria. In other words, community food growing comes in many shapes, sizes, and definitions.

HOW TO USE THIS BOOK

My intent is to provide guidance, best practices, advice, and suggestions that will help you create resilient community gardens—in all their incarnations—no matter where the community is. The story of your garden won't be a linear one. You may already have land to use or a community to serve. You may be brand new to the concept of organizing, or an old hand trying a new tactic to build community in the form of a garden. You may have no clue how to grow food, or you may be a Master Gardener.

This book is set up so you can jump into the section that is most relevant; you might just need some guidance on building the physical garden; or you might have a garden already and want some thoughts on boosting community involvement year-round or managing volunteers. You may be starting from scratch and need to read cover to cover before you develop a game plan for your would-be community garden. Here's what you'll find:

Chapter 1 outlines community organizing principles and provides a mission questionnaire to help you determine the motivation for the community garden. Case studies from successful garden programs in the United States and Canada illustrate how a mission-driven garden grows and flourishes as it meets the needs of the community. Chapter 2 provides agendas, worksheets, and tools to host successful meetings that will engage participants. Tips and tricks for effective leadership and group decision-making are offered. Chapter 3 includes important planning and design considerations, a framework for a successful group-design process, advice on budget development and working with contractors, and other factors key to building the physical garden. Chapter 4 highlights the business practices necessary for the long-term health of the garden organization, from fundraising to successful partnerships, and nonprofit status to liability. Chapter 5 focuses on positive management of gardeners and volunteers to build and maintain the garden, and chapter 6 provides fun ideas for events and activities to keep people connected to the garden year-round. Chapter 7 offers basic skills for teaching new gardeners, while chapter 8 provides valuable how-to information on sowing, growing, harvesting, and cooking twenty-one popular and easy-to-grow vegetables.

Starting a community garden is so much more than building raised beds and shoveling soil. The comprehensive advice provided in this book—which includes helpful planners and other reference sheets to copy and utilize as you create and build your community garden—is meant to help you understand all the essential facets of a successful, sustainable, long-term garden.

You are changing the world, after all. Might as well do it right.

PART ONE

GATHERING YOUR COMMUNITY

1. WITHOUT COMMUNITY, IT'S JUST A GARDEN

Getting Organized

Many people believe the heavy lifting—such as land acquisition and preparation, garden building, and soil shoveling—is the hard part of starting a community garden. Don't get me wrong! It takes a lot of physical labor to build a garden. But in reality, the toughest part is building the community first. The finite activity of the "stuff" of a garden is tangible; everyone can see the layout, the fence, the watering system. All is clear to the eye—"Ah, this is a garden!" But both seeing and navigating the intangible aspects of community are much more subtle and vital to the long-term success of the garden.

It is easy to get caught up in the excitement of spring—everyone wants to get their hands dirty and do some work—but without proper community structure, there's no assurance the garden will survive once the thrill of its newness is gone. Think of that admonition when you were a kid and your mother wouldn't let you get a puppy. Sure, it would be fun, but there's a lot of work required to enjoy the puppy kisses and tail wagging, and that dog might not be so cute when it grows up and needs a lot of maintenance. Without a community, a few months later you've just got a garden. And chances are, it is such a big garden that you or a few friends may not be able to maintain it for the long haul.

This is where community organizing comes into play. It is vital that the food-growing part of your project be the smallest part. How can that be if it's all about the garden? Yes, this is true—it is all about the garden, but perhaps in ways you don't understand just yet.

COMMUNITY ORGANIZING

What do you think of when you hear the phrase "community organizing"? Does it have a political meaning: protesting social injustice, unfair civic rulings—or does it make you think of "fighting the man"?

> *Organizing is what you do before you do something, so that when you do it, it is not all mixed up.*
>
> —A.A. Milne

LEADERSHIP VS. ORGANIZING

It is important to understand the difference between leadership and organizing. Oftentimes they are seen as the same thing, and the characteristics found in good leaders are often found in good organizers. But there is a crucial difference. Leaders create visions that people want to follow; and while that vision may require management and nurturing over time, it is a top-down scenario. Leaders are required to articulate their vision to move people in a specific direction.

Organizing, however, harnesses the power of consensus to create a shared vision and shared direction. The organizer's job isn't to push people toward his or her personal dream, but to foster a collective goal, to help build the community around that goal, and to inspire people to take on responsibility through action. This bottom-up approach is quite different than what I often see in our hierarchical world, and accordingly, it requires a different set of skills than many of us exercise on a daily basis.

Truth be told, your organization may need a little bit of both approaches. Some passionate soul may come up with a great idea for that empty piece of land in your neighborhood and his or her enthusiasm may attract others who buy into the dream. And while the vision is great, that visionary may or may not be a good organizer, so others—those who joined and believed in the dream—may need to step into the gap between the leader's vision and reality. Or you may be part of an organization in which there is no vision yet, but there's plenty of energy, and someone needs to step up to help shine a light down the collective path with his or her organizing ability. Organizing and leadership use different tactics, but as long as those tactics are being used toward a common goal, it's all good.

Does it have an organizational meaning—planning a food drive or a block party for your kid's school or your religious organization? Community organizing means a lot of things to a lot of people. When I began the Peterson Garden Project, I was new to the community-organizing world, but I found that my business management skills influenced my approach and helped tremendously.

The fact is, we all have some experience and perspective on aspects of leadership and community organizing, whether we call it that or not—be it planning an event, gathering signatures for a petition, managing a team, or any other scenario where a group of people need to move toward a common outcome. Everyone has either led or been part of a *successful* group—and everyone has either led or been part of an *unsuccessful* group. We all know how both scenarios feel—and, I would hazard to guess, we'd all rather spend our time in a successful group.

Ultimately, the long-term sustainability of any new garden organization is dependent on the garden being relevant and valuable to a variety of stakeholders. Effective organizing creates a culture of shared leadership, open communication, and agreed-upon processes.

CELEBRATE ASSET AWESOMENESS

There are college degrees and entire careers dedicated to community organizing. To keep it simple, I'll focus on one method that I believe is a concise, logical approach: Asset Based Community Development (ABCD)—or, as many call it, glass-half-full organizing. It's an approach that helps communities and groups focus on what they *do* have (assets based), instead of what they don't (needs based). The ABCD approach is very powerful because instead of creating anxiety about what a group may be lacking and need to find, finance, or work around, it celebrates what a group already has, helping members coalesce around those existing assets. ABCD encourages communities to rely on and celebrate their existing strengths.

Asset Based Community Development is an approach that encourages your community of gardeners to be active players and to pool assets. The principle has been used in community organizing scenarios for many purposes, from getting laws changed to addressing neighborhood challenges. In your case, the desired outcome is tangible—a vegetable garden that will become a fixture of the community. This type of organizing allows the outcome to be a true expression of the participants' efforts, values, and ideas. It can create meaningful and long-lasting change.

WHERE THERE IS NO VISION, THE PEOPLE PERISH: DEVELOPING A MISSION

That old verse may be a bit dramatic but it proves a time-tested point: without a common direction, nothing gets accomplished.

Regardless of the motivation to start a community garden, it is important at the very beginning for you and the team that emerges from your organizing work to define the collective vision. The mission may change over time, and that's okay, but by stating the reason for your community garden from the outset, you will have a framework to address all the key aspects of a healthy start: communication, community outreach, funding, rallying volunteers and neighbors, and more.

How Will Your Garden Serve the Community?

The first step toward creating a community garden is to discover and articulate the reason for starting it—to create your mission statement. This will help everyone involved understand what it will take for the garden to survive for the long haul. Motivations could include community building, social justice, food insecurity, or religious outreach. It might simply be an empty eyesore of a lot that's been bugging you and your neighbors for a long time. All reasons are valid and only your group knows the outcomes that will best impact the community.

The mission questionnaire contains a list of questions that the community can use to develop the garden's mission statement (the process of which is covered in chapter 2, where you'll find guidelines for what to include in your initial meetings). Collectively answering these questions will give the community as a whole an understanding of what the group can do with the garden space. There will be many possibilities and ideas presented, which then can be used as discussion points during organizational meetings, as you work toward a consensus on how the garden is going to serve the community. The mission will become the story of your garden, its origin myth, and formally articulating it with a mission statement in those seminal first meetings will help tremendously through the challenges and issues that will be encountered as the garden comes to life.

THE MISSION QUESTIONNAIRE

1. Are any existing organizations sponsoring or starting the garden? Do their missions need to be part of how the garden is developed?

2. Are funders sponsoring the garden? Do the funds dictate the garden mission in any way?

3. Does the garden location influence the mission? (For example, if the property is privately owned by an organization, their mission might impact what you are allowed to do on the property. If the property is owned by a city or municipality, does the land use require that it be open to the general public or unavailable to certain types of special interest groups?)

4. Does the garden mission or location influence the build? (Does proximity to a sponsor or partner dictate where the garden is? Does the type of garden, a garden where food is grown for donation for example, influence the type of garden to be constructed? Do added mission objectives such as meeting space or a teaching area influence construction?)

5. Who is the food being grown for? (Is the food to be donated to a nutrition program or used by an organization to feed people? Is the garden set up for families to grow the food for their own use?)

6. Who are the gardeners? (Is the garden open to everyone or focused on a specific group? For example, are the gardeners of all ages or a specific age group such as teens or the elderly?)

7. Does the neighborhood itself have any impact on the mission? (Will the garden deter crime? Bring neighbors together? Help with a food desert? Create green space?)

8. Is there an educational mandate for the garden? (Do the gardeners know how to grow food? Will this skill help them in other ways?)

9. Is the garden genesis driven by some other need, example, or force? (For example, a historical reference to the successful victory garden movement of World War II? A respected community member who dedicated their efforts to teaching or helping others? A community need or group?)

SIX SUCCESSFUL COMMUNITY GARDENS:
CASE STUDIES

Now that you've familiarized yourself with the questions, this section illustrates how a mission-driven approach helps to establish organizational best practices and direct decision making as organizations evolve over time. Your garden will be its own special place and will have its own story to tell. But by reading what others are doing, you may find inspiration or ideas for your own mission-driven garden.

PETERSON GARDEN PROJECT, CHICAGO, ILLINOIS

Are any existing organizations sponsoring or starting the garden? Do their missions need to be part of how the garden is developed?

While partnerships developed over time, initially there were no organizations sponsoring the garden so there was no need to incorporate others' objectives when the original garden was developed. This has changed over time as the program has expanded and new gardens have opened.

Are funders sponsoring the garden? Do the funds dictate the garden mission in any way?

The garden was funded by the gardeners themselves and donations from local businesses, so technically no funders. But this scenario did dictate that the program focus on being volunteer run since there were no funds to pay anyone. While the organization has grown, and hired one staff person to date (to manage volunteers!), the heart of the program is about people using what they have (empty city lots) to collectively learn a skill that will impact their families, neighborhoods, and the food system.

Does the garden mission or location influence the build?

Yes, the mission dictated how the garden was set up. The original Peterson Garden Project garden (and all subsequent gardens), are highly dependent on the mission for their construction. Considerations about the type of gardeners (busy city dwellers), the experience level (many with no experience), and the goal of teaching as many people as possible dictated how the garden was set up. This initial framework has provided a template for all subsequent gardens. And a surprising discovery that wasn't expected with the first garden was that this style, when replicated as closely as possible, allows for community garden development on a massive scale. Deviating from the plan has led to complexities that have become exponential and difficult to manage.

MISSION STATEMENT

The Peterson Garden Project is a volunteer organization committed to teaching people to grow their own food. They are based in Chicago, Illinois, where they build community vegetable gardens and stronger communities.

Does the garden location influence the mission?

Yes, the gardens are in high-density urban neighborhoods where people don't have the opportunity or room to grow their own food or learn how to do so.

Who is the food being grown for?

Food is grown by the participants for their own individual or family use. A program within each garden, called Grow2Give, works with volunteers to grow food for donation to food pantries located near the gardens.

Who are the gardeners?

The program is open to anyone who wants to become a member.

Does the neighborhood itself have any impact on the mission?

Yes. The original garden neighborhood was high density, so most participants had never had the chance to grow food before. This meant that people had to be taught how to grow their own food.

Is there an educational mandate for the garden?

Because so many Chicagoans had never had a place to grow food before, teaching this lifelong skill became the mission of the garden (and the organization that grew out of it). City land is very expensive and hard to procure, so the leadership team decided early on to put their energies into teaching as many people as possible, using unpurchased sites, rather than doing capital campaigns to buy land for a single long-term garden. In other words, focusing on long-term gardeners vs. long-term gardens.

Is the garden genesis driven by some other need, example or force?

The original garden was on the site of a victory garden during World War II. The history of the spot seemed a perfect background for recruiting a new generation of gardeners who were interested in growing food.

SAHARA SENIORS GARDEN, BRAMPTON, ONTARIO, CANADA

Are any existing organizations sponsoring or starting the garden? Do their missions need to be part of how the garden is developed?

A local project, the MIAG Center for Diverse Women and Families, partnered with Ecosource, a not-for-profit community environmental organization partnering with groups to start gardens, and received the grant to start the community garden. Punjabi Community Health Services is also a partner. The Sahara Seniors Garden project has a house on the property, sponsored by the Sikh temple; the house is used for indoor programs, and there is a garden at the back. Building raised beds was the initial main expense and part of the grant. Home Depot worked with the group to create a fence, which the store donated. The initial grant also allowed for a paid coordinator to get the garden off the ground. There are small donations from local businesses, including some transplants grown by local nurseries.

Does the garden mission or location influence the build?

The garden is in a suburban community with busy streets and almost no foot traffic, so a fence is a necessity. Many participants have to travel to get there, often walking, taking the bus, or riding a bike. It is important to have an indoor space as well as a garden, to keep the group together and active during the cold winter months. In the house, members prepare meals, attend programs on health and nutrition, and socialize. In the house's backyard, twenty-five raised beds have been built. Because the garden is located where the land was once cultivated as a farm, there are fruit trees on the property that have been revitalized by the community.

Does the garden location influence the mission?

The participating seniors are often isolated, even in their own homes and communities, as family members are either working or at school. Though many have to travel to get to the facility, working in the garden has had an overall positive effect on their health and well-being, and many of these senior members have a lifetime of farming experience. The building on the property allows the seniors to spend their non-gardening time attending programs, socializing, and preparing traditional meals from the produce they grow.

Who is the food being grown for?

The produce goes toward meals prepared at the center, to community meals at the Sikh temple, and is also taken home by the seniors to share with their families. Sharing the produce is important, as a free meal is available to anyone who comes to their temple (a tenet of their Sikh faith). Also, Meals on Wheels takes some of the produce for the community at large.

MISSION STATEMENT

The Sahara Seniors Garden in Brampton, Ontario, Canada, focuses on health, empowerment, and education in the local South Asian community.

Who are the gardeners?

Mainly the men tend the garden. Because the group is of an older generation, there is a fair amount of segregation and observance of traditions. Women helped with the design and creation of the raised beds, and sometimes garden, but generally the women prepare traditional meals using the vegetables. Two facilitators worked to start the garden and still come by on a daily basis, along with volunteer groups, including youth volunteers, who come in especially to help with tasks that might be difficult for older participants. A staff member coordinates the volunteers, an important and essential element for this community organization, so the volunteers are not overwhelmed and have a good experience working in the garden.

Does the neighborhood have any impact on the mission?

In the neighborhood where the Sahara Seniors Garden is located, the landscape is changing from farmland into suburban development. The sponsors were fortunate to obtain a property there with a building and a garden. Though many of the people who live in the area are from South Asia, most of the participating seniors come from farther afield to be part of their own cultural community.

Is there an educational mandate for the garden?

The educational mandate focuses on teaching healthy eating for older adults. Volunteers also teach the seniors how to build bird and pollinator houses. For both economic and educational reasons, the facilitators built a seed-starting setup in the house. Here the senior gardeners learn how to start seeds for favorite vegetables that are an integral part of their food traditions—vegetables such as tomatoes, melons, eggplant, and peppers, among others, as well as herbs unique to South Asian cooking.

Is the garden genesis driven by some other need, example, or force?

The Sahara Seniors Garden members celebrate their South Asian heritage through gardening. As a group they talk about food, patience, communication, and what it means to be a community. One of the garden founders and a facilitator, Carolyn, realized how much the seniors have to give back, and how happy the gardeners are when someone shows an interest. These garden members, along with the others in the partnership, encourage diverse cultural groups to interact and show an interest in one another, fostering the community-building process.

GROWING TOGETHER COMMUNITY GARDENS, FARGO, NORTH DAKOTA

MISSION STATEMENT

The mission of the three Growing Together gardens in Fargo, North Dakota, is to help refugees, bring churches together, eat well, and create community.

Are any existing organizations sponsoring or starting the garden? Do their missions need to be part of how the garden is developed?

Lutheran Social Services does resettlement of refugees in the United States. In 2006, their local church wanted to find a way to work on church property with the many refugees arriving in their community. The original garden land was bought by the church in Fargo. The Community Homes Garden, one of Growing Together's three gardens, is on city property owned by the park district. There they have a lease and pay no rent.

Are funders sponsoring the garden? Do the funds dictate the garden mission in any way?

All the land is donated and a local farmer tills the soil. The City of Fargo donates compost to augment the soil. Many donations to fund the gardens come through the Methodist and Lutheran churches, and the community at large is also supportive. Some funds come from employees of a local bank who receive $1,000 every year to give away. There is also support from local businesses, including the donation of boxes for packing produce. The garden leaders also get donation and funding results from putting a note in bulletins at the churches when they need supplies.

Does the garden location or mission influence the build?

The church garden is in a neighborhood where many of the refugees settled, and being able to walk to the church garden was important for these new Americans. The size of the Community Homes Garden (100 by 100 feet) on city property enabled the founders to work with the refugees to grow vegetables in a much larger space now serving twenty-five families. This garden is located on an unused baseball field in a low-income housing area. Each family has a 6-by-6-foot plot and receives two full bags of produce per week.

Does the garden location influence the mission?

The three gardens serve over a hundred refugee families, or "new American families," as founder Jack Wood likes to call his gardeners. Most participants need to be within walking distance of the gardens. Being close to a church basement enables the gardeners to grow 4,000 tomato seedlings each season.

Who is the food being grown for?

The produce goes to all the families who actively participate in the garden work. There are often three generations working in the gardens, with big families to feed. At the end of the season, they hold a garden market, raising about six hundred dollars from selling excess produce.

Who are the gardeners?
The gardeners are three generations of the one hundred "new American" families who are refugees from Bhutan, Africa, and Bosnia, sponsored by Lutheran Social Services. There are Buddhists, Hindus, and Moslems learning to garden together.

Does the neighborhood have any impact on the mission?
The mission is to bring the ethnically diverse people in the area together to garden as a community. To this end, it is important that the gardeners stick to a schedule, not coming and going from the garden at random. The three different generations are encouraged to become independent by gardening with their peers. People of multiple faiths spend three hours a week together in the garden, and bring people into the community to grow with them. Garden leaders work to break down caste systems from the countries of origin, and try to get women to speak for themselves, often by learning to design their own gardens.

Is there an educational mandate for the garden?
Many of the children of the refugees are actively involved in garden tasks at a garden called Growing Together at the Gathering. They learn to water, pick ripe vegetables, and box produce. In the garden is a Libraries for Everyone box with books for young children. Teacher volunteers help by working with the children in the garden and conducting a reading program. Once a week, children garden for an hour and read books for an hour. Then the group prepares a meal. A local bakery, Breadsmith, donates four loaves of bread. On sandwich night, the children help prepare the meal, roasting corn and making salads and sandwiches.

Is the garden genesis driven by some other need, example, or force?
Food is important but getting together is a fellowship.

TRI-NEIGHBORHOOD COMMUNITY GARDEN, NORFOLK, VIRGINIA

Are any existing organizations sponsoring or starting the garden? Do their missions need to be part of how the garden is developed?

One of the three garden founders approached an executive at the Service Technologies Corporation for a meeting about a 10,000-square-foot corner lot adjacent to the company's building. The garden founders—Atsuko Biernot, Joseph Filipowski, and George Ibarra—put together a proposal with a garden plan and a promise to give away the food that would grow there. The company donated the land.

Are funders sponsoring the garden? Do the funds dictate the garden mission in any way?

The garden received a donation of soil for raised beds from a nearby organic farmer, while local businesses donated tools. A car repair shop close to the garden offered to supply the water. Now that the garden is running successfully, there are a few garden "angels" who help when needed. For example, an angel stepped in and paid the water bill for the loan of water from the garage.

Does the garden location or mission influence the build?

A microclimate is created by the surrounding industrial buildings' bright white walls. The garden is in a commercial neighborhood with a low-income, mixed ethnic population dealing with food insecurity.

Does the garden location influence the mission?

Because of the neighborhood's food insecurity, there is no fence and the garden is open 24/7 to anyone who wants to harvest the vegetables. Harvested food is delivered to various charities, food banks, and soup kitchens serving the neighborhood. Every year the group goes on a few outings to help other people start a community garden, including a satellite garden a mile away near an elementary school on city property.

Who is the food being grown for?

The founding group of three puts into practice their progressive ideals on social and economic justice, giving away the bounty to anyone who comes by. One year they gave away fifteen hundred pounds of food, much of it going to families in need.

Who are the gardeners?

Many of the gardeners are individual families with no place of their own to grow food. Volunteers do everything and show up when they can. Monday is the dedicated gardening day; the three founders are always there, and up

MISSION STATEMENT

The Tri-Neighborhood Community Garden of Norfolk, Virginia, is a nonprofit effort manned by volunteers as a community–teaching garden, promoting a prosperous, equitable, and sustainable world.

to twenty people show up, many with their children. Brownie troops work in the garden to earn badges, children from the local YMCA help out, and students from Old Dominion University also volunteer. People from outside the neighborhood also come to work in the garden, thanks to word of mouth. These participants often become regular volunteers.

Does the neighborhood have any impact on the mission?

Because the garden is in an industrial area with an economically challenged population, the founders wanted everyone to have access to the produce, whether they put in time gardening or not. This means keeping the garden fence-free, with all the tools and equipment available for anyone to use. According to the locals, this policy has changed the area from a dangerous one to one in which people can walk around and garden night and day. With zero budget, the local residents are engaged in making whatever the garden needs, such as trellises and cold frames, from found or salvaged objects. Nothing is locked up; there are no rules.

Is there an educational mandate for the garden?

Because of the founders' attitudes, there is no formal structure or mandate in this community garden. But those neighbors working in the garden are learning how to grow their own food. And now they often take their knowledge to other communities and help them start gardens. The founders have also started a satellite garden for an elementary school, where the children are educated about organic gardening and composting.

Is the garden genesis driven by some other need, example or force?

The three garden founders are completely driven by their ideals around social and economic justice. Their explanation for starting the garden: "We wanted to do something to make a difference." In the garden, they show people that they don't need a lot of land or money to garden and grow healthy food. Right now they are exploring permaculture and a move away from formal, traditional gardening.

GUADALUPE MONTESSORI SCHOOL GARDEN, SILVER CITY, NEW MEXICO

Are any existing organizations sponsoring or starting the garden? Do their missions need to be part of how the garden is developed?

Garden founder Martha Egnal and other interested community members went to a local Earth Day celebration with a sign about starting a garden. The Montessori School director and board supported the idea of a community garden and donated the adjacent land with a water supply, because the concept fit with their philosophy of education. From the beginning, the school community rallied to make the garden a reality, and has been an active participant ever since. The school sees the garden as a mutually supportive relationship between their community and the larger community around them. Part of the Montessori doctrine encourages hands-on learning. The goal of the garden is to offer just that—not only for the students, but for the surrounding community as well.

Are funders sponsoring the garden? Do the funds dictate the garden mission in any way?

Most of the funding comes through small donations from this community with limited resources. A longtime local farmer helped them get going by working with Martha and one other person on the plan for the layout and on building a fence. They have received small grants from local enterprises and the National Gardening Association, and also hold fundraising events announced by the local radio station.

Does the garden location influence the build?

The garden is next to the school on school property, which was once a convent with a garden and vineyards. The garden was structured as a community garden with families from the area and the school working together.

Does the garden location influence the mission?

Produce from the garden is prepared for the school lunch program. Parents of children in the school and other community members often spend time working in the garden as part of their dedicated volunteer time. Every week, all grades work in the garden as part of their curriculum of nature-based activities. Learning about where what they eat comes from, and growing it themselves, is helping train the palates of these children to have a taste for real food.

MISSION STATEMENT

The mission of the Guadalupe Montessori School garden in Silver City, New Mexico, is to grow fresh fruits and vegetables for the school's lunch program, to provide a peaceful and carefully planned learning environment for students, and to strengthen the school's relationship with the community through education and entrepreneurial activities.

Who is the food being grown for?

Produce from the garden is used by the school for the lunch program, while the excess is sold at the local farmers' market, to restaurants, and to a food co-op. This is more about community outreach than actual profit.

Who are the gardeners?

The garden tasks are broken down so the students understand them and will be successful. Martha Egnal is the garden supervisor and has had invaluable help from an AmeriCorps member who worked with her for three years, enabling expansion of the garden in size and scope. Now the garden has a FoodCorps service member and is partnered with the Volunteer Center in town. There are workdays with a few dedicated volunteer families. Members of the community are asked to contribute their skills to the garden. Parents required to provide volunteer hours also work in the garden.

Does the neighborhood have any impact on the mission?

The vision is for the garden is to become a resource in a hard-pressed community—for people to learn about home gardening, raising small animals, beekeeping, food preservation, cooking, and nutrition. Garden leaders are also looking at needed youth programming; in the works are a new school that might be built for a variety of age groups, and the expansion of the program into agricultural production that would include skills and job training.

Is there an educational mandate for the garden?

Education in this garden is about balancing production with enrichment—and the need to be process oriented rather than just produce oriented. There are three levels of participation in the first through sixth grades. Every week children work in the garden, planting seeds and harvesting. Older children keep garden journals, observing one spot over time to identify bugs and plants, doing plant pressings, painting, and writing. The community members are also partners in the success of the garden and participate in the growing and education.

Is the garden genesis driven by some other need, example, or force?

Martha Egnal believes in the therapeutic value of cultivating a seed—to her, the potential benefits are huge. This garden founder felt something was broken about the food system. She has a passion for social change, and wanted a way to create social change peacefully, combining environmental work with a hands-on project that brought the community and the school together.

THE HOMELESS GARDEN PROJECT, SANTA CRUZ, CALIFORNIA

Are any existing organizations sponsoring or starting the garden? Do their missions need to be part of how the garden is developed?

The first organic garden was a program by the Citizens Committee on the Homeless, located on two acres of land owned by the city; it was a temporary location from the start, and, in 1995, the garden moved. The new spot was developed on three acres of private, donated land with a month-to-month lease.

Are funders sponsoring the garden? Do the funds dictate the garden mission in any way?

The Homeless Garden Project receives a small income through grants, donations from individuals, and earned income from a CSA (Community Supported Agriculture) and a farm stand. Feed Two Birds with One Worm is a funding program for donors to contribute money for shares that distribute food to low-income people in the community. The City of Santa Cruz has a master plan for a greenbelt that includes a nine-acre permanent site for the Homeless Garden Project, to be financed by a capital campaign.

Does the garden location influence the mission?

The garden was positioned to make it accessible for participants. As well as gardening experience, the members receive basic job training and transitional employment, so they need to be able to be at the three-acre garden as much as possible.

Does the garden mission or location influence the build?

There needed to be enough land for a structure to be incorporated for meetings and group lunches made from garden produce, two important elements of the Homeless Garden Project. There has been some vandalism as the garden is not fenced; the community responded with support when there were two fires that destroyed buildings, and Habitat for Humanity built a new structure.

Who is the food being grown for?

Many participants don't have a place to cook, or they might live in a shelter without these facilities. Shared lunches utilize the produce grown and the rest is sold at the local farmers' market or distributed through a CSA with members who pay a fee. These funding sources support the project. Produce is also made available to low-income community members.

MISSION STATEMENT

In the soil of our urban farm and garden, people find the tools they need to build a home in the world.

Who are the gardeners?

A diverse population of up to fifteen people who are mainly Asian, Mexican, and Native American, including several veterans, form the core of the program, with other community members working in volunteer capacities.

Does the neighborhood have any impact on the mission?

Only in that space was available and it was accessible to participants.

Is there an educational mandate for the garden?

The entire project is about education—both in growing food and in growing skills for participants to move out of homelessness.

Is the garden genesis driven by some other need, example, or force?

The founder, Paul Lee, is a visionary who wanted to move the homeless out of homelessness by helping them do something for the environment that they could be proud of.

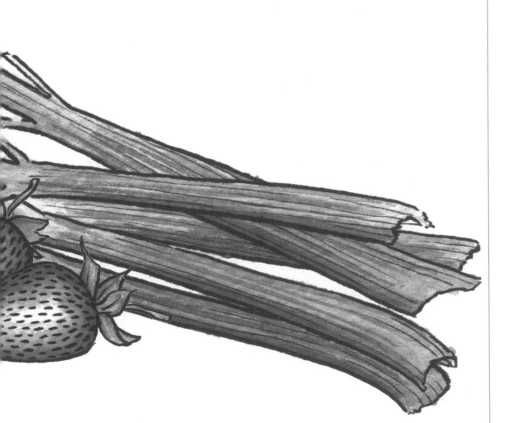

2. GET THE PARTY STARTED

Meetings with a Mission

My mother is a proponent of the "ounce of prevention" school of thought; I've found it's especially true when your garden community is just forming. Starting off on a solid foundation can go a long way toward simplifying things down the line.

If your garden is in the inception phase, follow the meeting planners in this chapter and chapter 3 for your initial community meetings. If your garden is already established, the planners will offer helpful tips to make your community organizing more effective.

Starting with a clean slate will help your group dream up the garden together during your first meetings. In reality, you and other interested parties may already have a list of tangible factors that will impact the future community garden. These givens, such as who owns the property, where the water source is located, or any limitations to land use, are useful pieces of information. You and others may have also already begun outreach and had discussions with neighbors and select individuals such as city officials and property or local business owners. All of this information is important to share, but before the planning train gets too far down the track, it is important to pull the community into the process. This way, all interested parties can define the outstanding issues together. This is the heart of community organizing: encouraging and empowering participants to make the decisions together and to combine their assets and talents to create the outcome they desire.

This chapter outlines a process for your initial meetings. I've broken it down into two meetings: the first focuses on introductions and getting to know the participants; the second focuses on developing the mission for the garden (the third meeting, on structural design, is covered in chapter 3). Depending on the dynamics of your group, you might be able to breeze through all three objectives in one meeting, or it may take many more. The important thing is having everyone

All the world's problems can be solved in a garden.

—Geoff Lawton

SPREAD THE WORD: A New Community Garden Is Forming!

An informational flyer is one simple and affordable method to get the word out. By placing it with neighborhood organizations, you get a chance to talk with potential partners (when you ask permission to post the flyer) and reach constituents.

Don't be shy about asking organizations or businesses if they'll include the announcement and meeting information in their newsletters or blogs, or on their Facebook pages. If you have some foot soldiers—such as neighbors, friends, local junior or high school students in need of service-learning hours—have them help deliver flyers to residences as well.

Places to Put Flyers

Religious organizations
Schools
Community centers
Senior centers
Local government offices
Libraries
Park field houses
Daycare centers
Newspaper offices
Restaurants
Health clubs
Office parks
Grocery stores
Medical offices

participate in the evolution of the garden—no matter how long it takes. Only you and your community will know the pace at which things should proceed. Trust your gut and use the following information as a guideline only.

TOOLS FOR SUCCESSFUL MEETINGS

If you're familiar with community organizing or have a job where meetings are the norm, some of this information is a no-brainer. If you're not, the tried-and-true meeting methods presented here will serve you well for any group meeting you need to conduct.

THE FIRST MEETING

You can't invite too many people to the first meeting. The more folks who know about the meeting and the interest in a community garden, the more assets and new friends you potentially have—people with skills that can help move the project along. It is imperative to give the members of the community in attendance—those who might be impacted by the future garden—a true sense of involvement in the garden's development, from the start. Some may decide not to attend future meetings, or to be involved in the garden at all, but they will at least know they have the option to participate.

Your first organizational meeting may be more introductory and social than anything else, and that is just fine. This is where all the players, interested individuals, and organizations gather to learn about each other and what each has to offer. As a group, participants will hear about the work so far to bring the garden into existence, as well as the givens that have been identified and established up to this point.

While it is important to get everyone introduced and up to speed on where the project is to date, don't rush things. If this first meeting is more about understanding the interested parties, so be it. A community isn't built in one meeting—the process takes time and work and patience. You can, however, set a great introductory tone for your new group by allowing plenty of time for participant sharing and input.

HOW TO HOLD A COMMUNITY MEETING

Before

➡ Secure the meeting space with convenient parking and access to public transportation; if it is wintertime, be sure to have a place to hang coats.

➡ Determine what elements you can add that will make participants comfortable. You'll need tables if there will be writing or drawing.

➡ Do you need an area for kids?

➡ Will there be coffee and refreshments?

➡ Advertise through as many channels as possible, allowing plenty of time for people to schedule the meeting into their calendars (at least three weeks in advance, preferably more).

➡ Provide the address, date, time, location, directions (if the location is difficult to find), and any other information that will make attendance a success.

➡ Include contact numbers and e-mail addresses in case people have questions beforehand or can't attend this particular meeting but want to be involved.

➡ Invite interested parties to be greeters; staff a sign-in table.

➡ Create an agenda to use while conducting your meeting (see pages 38 and 39).

➡ Decide on handouts, if any, and create them.

During

➡ Provide good signage so the meeting is easy to find.

➡ Make sure you collect contact information to create an interest list and to communicate with people after the meeting; this can be done at the sign-in desk or you can pass a sign-in sheet around during the meeting.

➡ Greet people. Thank them for attending. Welcome them.

➡ Take notes.

➡ Make helpers easy to identify via name tags or some other easy-to-spot item such as a T-shirt or hat.

After

➡ Send attendees a thank-you note or e-mail, a copy of the participant list, meeting notes, and any next steps decided on in the first meeting. Invite everyone on the interest list to the next meeting and encourage them to invite others as well.

➡ Solicit feedback in your thank-you and reply to all questions or comments that arise after the meeting.

The Agenda

There's no quicker way to lose interest with a group of people than by wasting their valuable time. An agenda is a vital tool to keep a meeting moving along on time and on task. It covers the items the meeting needs to accomplish and address. The following is an agenda template that I've developed over the years, which you can utilize as a road map. It can work for any of your meetings, though you may not need to include all the items for each meeting.

1. WELCOME

Your initial greeting sets the meeting's tone. Try to keep it upbeat. If you feel uncomfortable in front of people, ask someone who is outgoing to welcome guests.

2. OVERVIEW

State the goals of the meeting. This is also a good time to acknowledge any elephants in the room. For example, if a previous meeting became contentious, mention that the current meeting will address that conflict. Never be afraid to bring up issues within the group! Unspoken disagreements won't evaporate, and one of the aspects of a healthy group is successfully managing conflict.

3. GROUND RULES

Discuss the length of the meeting, how off-topic comments will be handled, and other group conduct issues. As your group gels, this section can be brief, but it's important if new people are attending a meeting for the first time. Yes, you may start to sound like a broken record, but it means there can be no excuses for bad behavior.

4. AGENDA REVIEW

If yours is an established group and you have distributed an agenda prior to the meeting, reviewing it is a general courtesy. It never hurts to ask if anything is missing, so the community has a chance to chime in, particularly at initial meetings. This is a good habit to get into for all meetings, because it levels the playing field and shows that the hosts are equal co-participants, not the sole deciders.

ANATOMY OF AN AGENDA

1. **WELCOME**
2. **OVERVIEW**
3. **GROUND RULES**
4. **AGENDA REVIEW**
5. **INTRODUCTIONS**
6. **ACTION ITEMS**
7. **RECAP**
8. **NEXT STEPS**
9. **CALENDAR**
10. **WRAP-UP**
11. **HANG OUT**

5. INTRODUCTIONS

At your first meetings, allow people plenty of time to introduce themselves. If your group is already formed, use this time to have guests introduce themselves. Be prepared! This will likely be the first time others have a chance to speak, and it can also be when personal agendas surface. Kindly remind attendees that this time is only for introductions, and restate the ground rules for off-topic issues.

6. ACTION ITEMS

These are the heart of the meeting—where the real work gets done. You may have one or several things you want to accomplish after introductions. Only you know what needs to get done. Often action items can be accomplished in a group discussion; sometimes small groups are required. If, as you're diving into the heart of the meeting, you are unclear about the best way to accomplish a list of action items, ask the group for feedback: Do they prefer discussion, small groups, or another approach?

7. RECAP

After completing action items, or when the meeting is winding down, assess anything left outstanding from the agenda. These topics can be agenda items for next time or, if they are time sensitive and the group agrees, they can be handled after the meeting. Give the group an opportunity to be part of the recap.

8. NEXT STEPS

These could include research, activities, or agenda items that require some work before the next meeting. When people volunteer, agree on a deadline, then follow up to make sure the task was accomplished, or provide what they need to finish the task. Remember, working together is fundamental to the success of the group and the garden—it is important that tasks are spread around and not heaped on a few people. If one or two people are doing everything, it's a sign that either other groups members aren't motivated, or that some might not be willing to share the workload (or maybe a combination of both).

9. CALENDAR

Coordinating schedules for any group will make you want to pull your hair out. There is never a good time for everyone, so figure out what works for the majority and get it on the calendar now. If calendars seem particularly impossible for your group, and there's enough momentum on a particular issue or topic, you might suggest scheduling small-group get-togethers before the next organizational meeting. That way, one or two small-group representatives can report back if the entire small group is unable to attend.

10. WRAP-UP

This is the time to say thank you—the most important phrase in the world! Volunteer community members do things out of the goodness of their hearts—recognize that, thank them, and set a positive, grateful tone for your next meeting.

11. HANG OUT

The time immediately after a meeting can be as effective as the entire meeting. Plan on spending a few minutes after the wrap-up to answer questions, interact, and listen.

FEEL THE LOVE
Agenda for the First Community Meeting

The first meeting accomplishes a lot of important things. You start to establish group norms with which participants can be comfortable; you present a meeting format that can become familiar and easy to replicate for other group leaders; and, most importantly, your organization and efficiency set a tone for a productive group environment.

➡ WELCOME
Introduce yourself and any teammates or special guests who are leading or attending the meeting, and thank people for coming.

➡ OVERVIEW
Briefly state the purpose of this meeting, that it is related to a community garden project. Report any relevant information, such as a specific property that has been identified, or support from local officials. Share any other pertinent issues that arose prior to this first meeting.

➡ GROUND RULES
Discuss meeting length, how off-topic comments will be handled, and anything else you want to say about group-participation approaches. Now might be a good time to share the Attributes of a Successful Group (p. 44), either by way of a handout or writing them on large easel paper.

➡ AGENDA REVIEW
At this first meeting, ask participants to quickly review the agenda and share any items that need to be added.

➡ INTRODUCTIONS
Depending on the number of attendees and the amount of time you have for the meeting, try to allow everyone a chance to introduce themselves. If there are collectives or sub-groups in attendance, ask a representative from each group to state his or her name, the names of colleagues who are present, the group's name, its mission, and a brief statement about their interest in the garden.

➡ ACTION ITEM(S)
The action item for this first meeting is to help people get to know each other and start taking ownership of the community garden. Right off the bat, they should be thinking about what or how they can contribute. If you are following the Asset Based Community Development approach discussed in chapter 1, give a brief overview of that approach before the breakout.

➡ RECAP
After you've completed your action items, assess anything left outstanding from the agenda. These things can be considered as agenda items for next time. Be sure to allow the group plenty of opportunity to add to the recap.

➡ NEXT STEPS
If applicable, assign next steps to attendees. Your breakout exercise may uncover a variety of talents that can help make the next meeting easier and more group driven. Next steps could include deploying some of this talent for research or activities needed to make the following meeting effective.

GETTING PEOPLE TALKING: THE BREAKOUT

Keep in mind that our world is very top-down, so you may need to encourage participants to articulate their wants, needs, and talents, and how they can contribute to creating the garden (vs. having it created for them).

Have attendees break into small groups; the size and number depend on the number of participants. Generally, six to eight people per group works well. Give each group twenty to forty-five minutes to discuss the following:

➡ **Motivations** they or their organization have about a community garden

➡ **Pros and cons** for the community

➡ **Any assets** they or their organization can contribute to the garden

When time is up, have the small groups reconvene into the larger gathering, with one representative reporting each group's answers.

Ask someone to record the group responses on a large flip chart. You can have four category headings: Motivations, Pros, Cons, and Assets.

There are no right or wrong answers in breakouts; they provide a time for thoughts to begin percolating collectively and for different perspectives to be expressed—all of which produces food for thought for future meetings. If this exercise creates a feeling that things are hanging in midair without a conclusion, that's okay, too. You can't solve everything in one meeting and shouldn't expect to. The point of this exercise is to get people talking and, hopefully, to begin revealing motives and resources.

➡ **CALENDAR**

Check schedules—and the seasonal calendar. If it's late in the spring, for example, you may need to meet quickly (within the next few weeks). If seasonal considerations aren't as pressing, plan to meet again four to six weeks out (that lets you continue to invite people who may not have been able to make the first meeting). Remember that small-group get-togethers can happen in the meantime, with a representative reporting back at the next large meeting.

➡ **WRAP-UP**

Time to thank everyone and express appreciation for their interest. Announce details of what will be covered in the next meeting based on the recap, and add that it will be a working session around development of the garden mission (if you've gotten to that point.)

➡ **HANG OUT**

Was your first meeting really exciting? Are people fired up to create this garden? If people can hang around and visit, let them. Or if you want to move the meeting to a nearby restaurant or bar for more socializing, that's great. A more social environment may provide a comfortable place for that quiet-but-powerful group member to be heard.

SUPPORT DIVERSITY

The community in your garden should reflect the community in the surrounding neighborhoods. Make sure to reach out to, and include, all the populations your neighborhood supports. This may take extra time and effort, and you may have to adjust communication methods to accommodate different languages and cultural approaches, but the work will pay off with a truly well-rounded and strong community that reflects the values of your neighborhood. For years, community gardens have been places where minorities and other cultural groups gather to celebrate their heritage and support each other emotionally and financially, by providing access to fresh, healthy food and a safe environment. As community gardens become more popular, it is important to not just consider a garden as something trendy or fun to do. Understand the power of community gardens to bring people together (which helps break down cultural barriers), and, as people grow food together, to establish common ground.

In addition to cultivating diversity, community gardens bring together people from other backgrounds, particularly immigrant populations, who have experience growing food. Some may have been farmers in their native lands. Besides having an opportunity to cultivate food again, people who have been displaced from an agricultural past are also great resources as teachers and mentors for new gardeners. Language can sometimes be a barrier, but the visual, living garden—and the fact that everybody eats—can go a long way toward a shared understanding.

Small-Group Breakouts

You want participants to be as comfortable and open in meetings as possible. Some folks don't have a problem addressing a large group. Many do. To get people talking, warmed up, and, ultimately, contributing to the meeting, breaking the larger group into smaller units can be an effective tool.

Small groups are also great for sorting people by their interests. Members can self-select the small groups or committees where they'll contribute the most, and this is also where committee work can happen.

An easy way to get a good mix of people in each group is to count off. Starting at the front right or left of the room, have people count from one to however many groups you will have; if you want five groups, they'll count from one through five, then start again with one until everyone is assigned a number. Sort people into their numbered groups for further discussion. This is also a good trick to get people who came together separated and meeting others.

Tricks for Keeping Meetings on Topic

When addressing situations that may derail the agenda, you can suggest that items not on the agenda be put in "the parking lot"— or, as known in greener circles, "the bike rack"—to be addressed later. These can be anything that is beyond the scope of the agenda, too complex, or may require more time than has been allotted. Putting items on hold for later is also a great tool for managing attention-hogging personalities or disagreements within the group that escalate beyond polite conversations.

In some meetings, lots of topics get put on hold and "bike rack" becomes a verb (as in "Let's bike rack that topic for now"). Whatever you call it, by stating up front that this approach will be a course of protocol in your meetings, everyone not only understands the rules but can also speak up when the discussion is veering off course.

Items put on the bike rack can be part of the notes that are being taken, or you can have a separate large flip chart with the words Bike Rack at the top, and make a list as the meeting progresses. Just make sure bike-racked items are reiterated before the end of the meeting, perhaps in your recap. Also briefly address how they will be approached (such as in a small working group or as an agenda item) at the next meeting.

The bike rack can be a great thing—don't be surprised if it reveals a lot about the group's understanding (or misunderstanding), personalities, and even underlying goals or challenges.

First Meeting Pitfalls

Don't get tactical too fast. It is really easy to jump in and start talking about the number of beds the group will build, whether there will be a storage shed, where the water will come from, and so on. And, if you've kicked off the meeting with a list of givens, that just adds fuel to the fire. This is really fun stuff! But it is premature. The goal of your first few meetings is to introduce people to each other, help them understand what the group has to offer, and, collectively, to start forming the vision of the garden.

You will, no doubt, have some hard chargers at the meeting who have built gardens or been part of a community garden before and *want to get it done!* It is great to have these people around and important not to dampen their enthusiasm, but first things first. Take time to understand the why of the garden before you dive into the how. Feel free to discuss these points in the Overview or Ground Rules section of your meeting.

Don't be surprised by other agendas. An agenda is a great tool to keep people on topic, but the word has a double meaning. Often, particularly where community assets are concerned, attendees may show up with other agendas, which won't be about the garden at all. This can be subtle or overt. These individuals may see this gathering as a chance to be heard on another issue. Particularly if you have local government officials or other people with authority present, they may take the opportunity to address things beyond the scope of, or completely unrelated to, the potential garden.

There may be disruptive participants. Community projects often bring out people with lots of opinions. Opinions are good—and welcome!—as long as there is respect for the group. You might find individuals who monopolize the conversation or, on the extreme end, have outbursts that are not productive or relevant and make the group uncomfortable. Your first option is to table the issue, and kindly ask the disrupter to let others speak their piece. The second option is to ask the disrupter to leave the meeting. If that doesn't work, enlist the power of the group and vote him or her off the island. If all else fails and things get really out of control, end the meeting or call 911. (Hopefully, you will never run into this situation, but if you do, at least you'll be prepared!)

HANDOUT HINTS

There are several philosophies regarding handouts at meetings. Generally speaking, as soon as you hand something out, you will lose the attention of the group as they start reading whatever you've given them. A good rule of thumb is to pass around simple handouts that don't need explaining at the start of a discussion (such as agendas with limited text), and distribute more complex materials only as part of an exercise, after you've had a chance to introduce the topic. For example, if you have a text-heavy document you'd like attendees to read for a breakout exercise, hand it out *just prior* to the exercise and make reading it part of the breakout. If you have general materials that are important but not relevant to the meeting agenda, leave them on a table for people to pick up as they leave.

ATTRIBUTES OF A SUCCESSFUL GROUP

As your community develops over time, keep these characteristics of a successful group in mind and work toward having them form the backbone of your organization. A positive, productive team is important. If people aren't engaged and invested, they will either go away or become ineffective.

⇒ Everyone is working toward a shared goal: the garden mission.

⇒ The group has agreed-upon norms of behavior, and has taken the time to arrive at these norms collectively.

⇒ The group gets things done; they have a list of milestones and they actively work to accomplish them.

⇒ People are comfortable around each other.

⇒ Everyone participates in the conversations.

⇒ People's feelings are as welcomed as their ideas.

⇒ General agreement fuels decisions, and dissent is heard and respected, not pushed aside.

⇒ Members keep their promises.

⇒ Disagreement and critical opinions are not seen as negative; expressing an opposing view is relatively comfortable.

⇒ Leadership shifts among a number of individuals.

THE SECOND MEETING

You've laid the groundwork at your first successful community meeting. A set of group norms is starting to form, you know many of the potential players (and pitfalls), the community's assets are starting to show themselves, interest has been sparked, and people are engaged. The goal of the next meeting is to funnel all that energy and information into creating the garden's mission statement —or at least to work in that direction. The mission questionnaire discussed and provided in chapter 1 will be your road map. The discovery process could take a few meetings, though, and that's fine. Just work toward the goal with the group, reminding them that the questionnaire will help in the formation of the new community's all-important mission for the garden.

Understanding the Importance of the Mission Statement

A mission statement or, as it is sometimes called in the business world, an elevator pitch, is a quick, descriptive paragraph about an organization. It should be brief (no more than about five sentences), to the point, and ideally short enough to memorize.

This might seem like a silly exercise. It isn't. It is fundamental to your organization. By having a consensus-driven mission, you not only have buy-in from the community, earned through valuable discussion and group learning, you also have a reference point for the future.

If, down the road, individuals or a group join the community and have a different vision for the garden, you can point to the mission statement as a guiding principle or, if things have changed over time, reflect on the original mission statement as a discussion point for evolution.

One of the great things about a community deciding things together is that it generates a lot of good ideas. Of course, so many ideas may also be a challenge; you can only do so much with the available time, dollars, and energy. This makes understanding the mission of your garden all the more important—your mission can help channel all those thoughts, ideas, and passions toward a unified goal.

A mission statement can also protect you from rogue or out-of-scope ideas that might arise. If it is stated that the mission of your garden is growing food for others, that clarity and specificity will help you if someone jumps in and wants to start a for-profit urban farm on part of the garden space. You can politely decline on the grounds that it is contrary to your mission. Or if a community member really wants an elaborate, and costly, pergola or other structure, you can point out that the dollars and resources spent toward such a structure, while lovely, detract from the ultimate mission of the garden.

Additionally, your mission will impact the scope and types of partnerships you choose to pursue or perhaps the types of funding for which you can apply. If your garden's mission is teaching families about nutrition in order to decrease obesity and improve health, a partner selling unhealthy food products is probably not a good fit—and your mission has pre-defined that for you.

MARCHING ORDERS
Agenda for the Second Community Meeting

You're getting good at this agenda format by this point. Much of it will seem familiar and you can extemporize in each section as needed. You may not need to address all the categories, and that's okay, just remember the format should be used as a relevant template for all community meetings to establish order and organization. Include as many of the agenda items as are applicable.

➡ WELCOME
Introduce yourself and any teammates or special guests who will be leading or attending the meeting. Thank people for coming. If something funny or memorable happened at the first meeting, recount that positive event to rekindle the good feelings and outcomes.

➡ OVERVIEW
Reiterate the outcomes of the first meeting and state the purpose of this second meeting: fleshing out the mission of the garden. This is a good time to remind people that we're not to the garden building stage just yet—we're focusing on motives and mission first.

➡ GROUND RULES
Cover meeting length, how off-topic comments will be handled, and any other information about group participation. You might want to revisit the Attributes of a Successful Group (p. 44).

➡ AGENDA REVIEW
Ask participants to quickly review the agenda and to suggest any items that need to be included.

➡ INTRODUCTIONS
If the group composition is similar to the first meeting, have everyone quickly restate their name and the organization they represent (if any). If there are new participants, ask them to introduce themselves and, if applicable, their organization, and to give a brief overview of their interest in the garden.

➡ ACTION ITEM(S)
The action item for this second meeting is to work toward a mission statement and name for the garden.

➡ RECAP
Reiterate what everyone has agreed on during the meeting and recite the mission statement if you've gotten to a final stage.

➡ NEXT STEPS
If applicable, assign next steps to attendees.

➡ CALENDAR
Find a time for the next meeting or reiterate a pre-determined date.

➡ WRAP-UP
People may be both energized and tired from this exercise. Now is an important time to recognize the hard work it's taken to get to this point. All the discussion, effort, and ideas that went into this process are the foundation of your community. Congratulate yourselves!

➡ HANG OUT
If you have time, socialize afterward, so people can process the meeting. It could be the first time some participants have taken part in something like this, and a chance to decompress might be appreciated.

DEVELOPING THE MISSION STATEMENT

PART 1: THE MISSION QUESTIONNAIRE AND GARDEN NAME

Have attendees break into small groups and hand out the questionnaire. The size of each group depends on the number of attendees; six to eight people per group, generally.

Give each group twenty to forty-five minutes to discuss and fill out one mission questionnaire (p. 20). Remind everyone that there are no right or wrong answers. It is up to the group to decide the mission of the garden, and the process they use to get there is powerful, important, and just as valuable as the outcome itself.

If your garden doesn't already have a name, suggestions might pop up. Ask each group to discuss names and agree on the top two.

When time is up, ask groups to reconvene into the larger gathering, with one representative from each group reporting answers.

Ask someone to record the group responses on a large flip chart. Have one flip chart sheet for each of the nine questions and a tenth sheet for possible garden names. Vote on a garden name to get things rolling.

You will start to see themes emerge from the mission statement answers. You may also see conflicts of interest. Don't stress out! As a community organizer, it isn't your job to interpret or judge the decisions of the community, but to funnel their viewpoints toward consensus.

PART 2: MISSION STATEMENT MAD LIBS

Once you've reviewed all the answers, it is time to meld them into a cohesive mission statement.

Be prepared: people will get hung up on grammar, punctuation, and particular words (have a dictionary and thesaurus handy), and may end up overlooking the bigger point of the exercise. This is human nature and you'll just have to work through it. The group will go through an iterative phase, one idea spurring another. All types of group discussion are necessary to get to the right place. Luckily, time taken to work through answering the mission questionnaire will give a jump-start to forming the mission statement.

On a blank flip-chart page, write out the following statements and then fill in the answers, guiding the discussion toward consensus. You may want to pin up the original answer sheets. Work to blend the answers until the right phrasing for each emerges.

We are in partnership with:
(question #1 or #2 if applicable or desired)
Impacts that apply to our garden:
(question #3 or #4 if applicable)
Our purpose is to grow food for: (question #5)
Our gardeners are: (question #6)
Our garden is built to help our neighborhood:
(question #7 if applicable or desired)
Our goal is to teach:
(question #8 if applicable or desired)
We are inspired by: (question #9 if applicable)

Once all the responses are filled in, you'll have the basic elements to move toward a mission statement. If things veer off course, bring everyone back to the answers you agreed upon as a group. The closer you get to a final statement, the more you will likely have to fiddle with wording. Brace yourself, this might take a while! But you will all feel a gratifying sense of accomplishment when you are finally able to articulate your garden's mission statement!

Was that successful? I hope so. If not, you might have some more work to do to get to consensus within your group. Have you heard that expression, "How do you eat an elephant? One bite at a time."? As your group works through issues big and small, it will get easier and faster as group norms start to take shape.

Getting to Agreement

If, after the breakout sessions, you have a list of potential conflicts or sticking points, there's no option but to talk them through, one by one. The discussion will be invaluable for the cohesion of your group. Try to find common ground and then whittle away at an issue. You want to feel a sense of accomplishment at your meetings, and work toward the attributes of a successful group. If you have a list of things people disagree on, tackle the easiest ones first. As the group succeeds in coming to consensus, respect builds; when you get to more difficult matters later, members will understand how the group thinks and, hopefully, respect each other enough to listen to differing points of view.

If people become hot tempered or the conversation deteriorates, it is okay to put it on the bike rack for another meeting. If you or the other organizers are ever uncomfortable, it is okay to ask the group how to proceed—take a vote! Group consensus is the point, and a healthy group needs to deal with *all* matters—not just the pleasant stuff—collectively.

If you've gone through a session where you started with a mountain of disagreements and ended up with a molehill, recognize this hard work. Discussion and consensus take time and are sometimes uncomfortable for people. Acknowledge the effort put forth so far and take a moment to congratulate yourselves, because this is real progress!

If you have one or two remaining sticking points that really matter to a few individuals (and if personalities seem to be involved), have them agree to meet separately in a small group to discuss issues and report back to the group. Perhaps the time together will ease the conflict. This also spares group members from having to be bystanders to a potential power play. Everyone can comment or vote on the outcome at the next formal meeting.

Humanity on Parade

Communities are amazing things. Human nature at its best—and sometimes worst—is on display at group meetings, and people's passions, styles, fears, and dreams can influence, and sometimes direct, the life of the collective. Each group is different; perhaps every time you meet, a new member or idea changes the dynamic. Here are some ideas on how to be a good leader or team member, how to keep perspective, and how to *always* keep the glass half full.

How to be a Good Leader

Yes, you're organizing, but you also may find yourself in a leadership position. The composition of your group may require both leadership and organizing skills. This is a list of a few things you and others who are in the forefront of the community can do to be the people everyone wants on their team.

⇒ Have an open mind

⇒ Leave your ego and preconceptions at home

⇒ Acknowledge and celebrate the contributions of the team

⇒ Treat all ideas as valuable

⇒ Be a good listener

⇒ Begin with the end in mind

⇒ Make sure everyone leaves the meeting in a better place than when they arrived

As the leader of the group (who has likely already put in a lot of independent work getting the garden to this point), you may need to temper your personal desires or agenda, but of course, as a member of the community, your opinions do matter. Just be aware that your views can appear to have more weight in the group process. It is important to vocalize that you consider yourself a group member— subject to, and part of, group decisions, just like everyone else.

API

During a training I participated in once, the group was building the ground rules, or how they would behave collectively during their time together. At one point, a woman stood up to speak her piece, and said, "A-P-I." She let those three letters hang in the silent air for a moment while we all racked our brains to determine if we knew what the acronym meant.

Finally, she smiled one of the most beautiful smiles I have ever seen and said, "Assume Positive Intentions." That moment created a radical shift in how I thought about group interaction. Having come from the corporate world, which is often leader driven, contentious, and rife with personal agendas—the what's-in-it-for-me mentality—

I immediately liked this generous approach. It has changed my thinking for the better, about everything.

If you keep API in mind, it completely changes how you perceive, for example, that fellow group member who may be upset about the hose situation in the garden. It's not an attack on you—they simply want to keep their garden well watered (and maybe they're worried about everyone else's gardens, too). By assuming the best in every interaction, you can look beyond what might seem a threatening reaction or assault on the goals of the organization (or your goals for the day) and understand that some personal styles only appear confrontational. Maybe they're uncomfortable asking for things; maybe they are upset. It's likely that the focus is not on you but something more internal, perhaps a feeling of being prevented from making progress, a high overall stress level, or discomfort with not being able to find a solution without help.

R-E-S-P-E-C-T

Hum that iconic song together with me now.

We all know how to spell it, but do we know how to exercise it? One of the fundamental principles of organizing (and life in general) is respect for the ideas, opinions, and wishes of others. This is particularly true in community organizing, and is essential to the process. By respecting everyone's ideas, we can get to the heart of what we have to work with. People will have great ideas and some can be easily incorporated; other times their ideas will be contrary to the overarching goal of the group. By collecting, respecting, and discussing all the ideas forming the collective vision, everyone is engaged and feels part of the process.

Communicate, Communicate, Communicate!

People don't like surprises and they don't like feeling left out. You cannot overcommunicate as your group is starting out. Make open and frequent interaction a key strategy in your organizational playbook.

Also, you don't need to feel responsible for interpreting communications. If there's an issue, don't sugarcoat it or feel you need to manage or mitigate it. Let the community know the issue and let them find the solution. What the community comes up with may be what you thought would be a good solution all along, but don't cheat the community of the chance to arrive at the answer on their own.

Be sensitive to how you are communicating. People receive information in many ways, and you will have to employ a variety of tactics to effectively reach everyone in the group. While younger gardeners may like to get information through Facebook or Twitter, older gardeners may prefer to see things in print (flyers) or have a phone number to call for information. There is also a technology gap between the haves and the have-nots, so don't assume everyone has e-mail or computer access. Make sure your communication channels reach all potential gardeners, to guarantee your garden is a true reflection of the community's diversity.

As your community grows and the people get to know each other better, you'll find a balance of how and what to communicate. You won't need to share every small situation in the garden. Perhaps committees can be developed and empowered to oversee specific parts of the garden, so they can manage certain issues as they arise. You'll find a good balance between relevant communication and too much information. At the onset, however, *over*communication will convey that sharing information and the collective opinion matters.

Listen, Listen, Listen!

If the garden is truly to be a reflection of the community, then communication has to be a two-way street. As mentioned previously, people don't like surprises or being left out. They also need to feel their opinions matter. This is where leadership and organizing really come into play.

There are two types of listening: listening in order to reply and listening in order to understand. If a member presents an issue, and, as you listen, you are merely formulating a rebuttal in your head, you're not really listening. If you're listening to understand, you might not have an answer, and you can tell your fellow member that. By providing a place where people can air their views and really be heard, you're building an environment of respect.

I've found that one of the most powerful answers to a question I cannot answer is, "I don't know. What do you think?" People are so smart! Often folks who come up with questions already have a good answer—or the start of a good answer. Empower them to solve problems or to engage others in the solution.

Keep Agreements

Deadlines, to-dos, action items—whatever you want to call your commitments, it usually means that someone is supposed to do something by a date, or before someone else can do his or her part. One of the toughest things for a community to manage is people doing what they promise to do. As a leader of the organization, you need to set a good example in this area and encourage others to do the same.

When to Put the Smack Down

The act of talking about stuff feels good. Making spreadsheets, talking about stuff some more, planning to plan—all of these engage peo-

PARTNERSHIPS MAY COME IN SURPRISING PACKAGES

You will be amazed by the organizations or businesses in your community that can be effective partners. There are the obvious ones—hardware or lumber stores, garden centers, and community organizations—but sometimes partners might surface in unexpected places.

In Indianapolis, a local group, Urban Patch, created the OASIS program to address their food access issue in a unique way. OASIS partnered with the Fall Creek Gardens Urban Growers Resource Center to focus on food availability and environmental justice.

The garden, in the Mapleton-Fall Creek neighborhood, is located in a food desert—an area lacking accessibility to fresh, affordable, nutritious food—and the community was suffering. Most of the grocery stores in the neighborhood had moved out and dollar stores had moved in. Instead of fighting the trend, Urban Patch and the dollar stores in the community realized they had a common goal.

To fight the effects of the food desert, the dollar stores started carrying basic food staples. In addition to providing fresh food for the community, the collaboration of the three entities (Urban Patch, Fall Creek Gardens, and the dollar stores) evolved into a partnership that provided educational opportunities to community members. Participants were taught basic nutrition and cooking skills using low-cost staples, as well as where to get affordable foods and recipes. The dollar stores then shared the recipes and posted them on the shelves with their advertising.

Working together with limited and imperfect resources, the OASIS program has forged a partnership in which everyone benefits: the program fulfills its mission, the dollar stores make a profit and provide a service to the community, and community members have access to both the products and information they need to make smarter food decisions. A win, win, win situation.

ple. But it is possible to talk things into the ground without anything getting accomplished. This is when death by committee becomes a threat, and someone has to jump in and move things along. Deadlines can help, but someone—either you or another team leader—may need to hold people accountable and get things rolling again.

Practice What You Preach

Whatever the group agrees to, you as a leader and community member need to respect those wishes and comply with them. Being a leader does not give you special privileges—at least not in a highly functioning community setting. The rules apply to everyone. Period. You need to set a good example in your words and actions.

THE EXTENDED TEAM: FRIENDS AND PARTNERSHIPS

We've talked a lot about harnessing the ideas and enthusiasm of the individuals involved in your garden, but let's not overlook the power of partnerships.

If your garden is to have a social mandate of any kind, there is probably a nearby charitable, civic, or community organization or social service that could be a potential partner. Partnerships can be as minimal as like-minded people helping to spread the word about the garden program, or providing a potential volunteer pool to property owners who might provide space, resources, or support for your garden. No doubt, outside groups also have their own agendas, but if you can find the sweet spot where missions intersect, this can be a powerful foundation for the success of all involved parties.

There are many excellent reasons to partner with an established organization, but one of the greatest benefits is a built-in community that may be interested in the garden. Plus, they have the communication channels to reach out to their members directly. By sharing your communication needs with a partner organization, you not only get the benefit of their knowledge and enthusiasm, but also access to their participants.

It is very easy to be one-sided with partnership (or sponsor) relationships. You need something and they have it (clout, connections, land, supplies). Being selfish isn't going to help with long-term relationships. You need to consider what their wants, needs, and goals are as well, and work toward mutual success.

Also understand that partnerships take time. You may need to do a small project together before a partner is willing to take a big step with your group. Choose something that you know your organization can do successfully and keep your promises. This is important with everything you do, not just initial projects with partners. But, as your relationship develops, you'll understand how to work together and cut each other a little slack if things don't always go according to plan. Partnerships are like any other relationship—it takes time to work out the kinks. Expect this and don't rush the process.

THE RECIPROCITY MAP:
A PARTNERSHIP BREAKOUT

A great exercise to do with your community or partners is to explore a reciprocity map. This discussion tool helps illustrate how the partnership will benefit everyone. To help your community brainstorm potential partners, you can conduct this discussion in the now-familiar small-group breakout format. Or you can use this tool as an exercise in meetings with potential partners. All the rules of communicating, listening, and respect apply to partnerships, too. The more chances you have to truly interact and develop your partnership face-to-face, the more successful that relationship will be in the long run.

The illustration on the following page show a sample reciprocity map, and illustrates how partner relationships are a two-way street. In the sample, you'll see some defined benefits for each group. Your partnerships will be completely different. This sample is only meant to get you thinking about what you want from a partnership and how, by focusing on the benefits to both sides, the partnership is more powerful and mutually beneficial.

As with community meetings, taking some time to work with your partners to fill out the reciprocity map will create valuable dialogue and bonding that will serve as a strong foundation for your relationship. Copy the accompanying blank template as a starting point.

Reciprocity maps illustrate mutual benefits between partners.

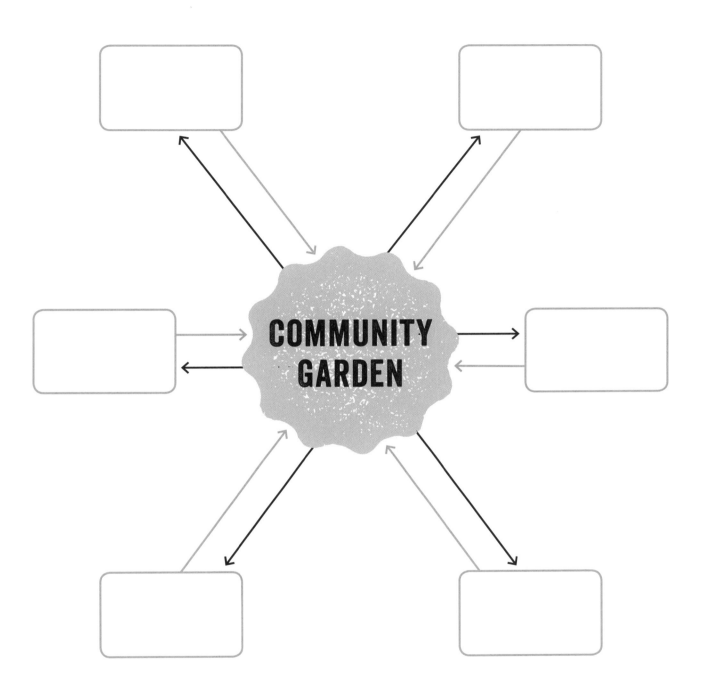

COMMUNITY GARDEN

Use a reciprocity map template to identify your garden's potential partnerships.

SUPPORT STRUCTURES

 # 3. BRINGING THE GARDEN TO LIFE

Planning and Design

Every county, municipality, town, and city has its own approach to supporting and regulating community gardens, which someone in your group will have to research and learn. These support systems, if they exist, will be one of many factors to be taken into account as the garden plan evolves. There are a lot of physical elements that need to be securely in place for a new garden to flourish. The mission-building work you have done as a group and your group's motivations for starting the food garden will influence and direct your decisions on how the physical garden becomes a reality.

Show me your garden and I shall tell you what you are.

—Alfred Austin

PLANNING

There are many factors that need to be considered when planning your garden. If you already have a site identified, congratulations! That's one of the hardest parts. If you don't have a site identified, the first and biggest task for your team is to identify and secure land with a convenient water source and enough sun for growing vegetables. After you have these biggies out of the way, focus your planning on the garden type, soil, supplies and amenities, security, and any building materials you may need for the type of garden your community envisions.

Site Location

If there are no established organizations to help with your program, or if for some reason you need to go rogue to execute your community's vision, there will be challenges developing the infrastructure for your community food garden. Land and water are generally the largest obstacles.

THE EASY PATH

The simplest way to get your garden going is to plug into a support organization that already has a system for developing gardens, such as Denver's DUG (Denver Urban Gardens), Seattle's P-Patch, New York City's Green Thumb, Austin's Sustainable Food Center, and Chicago's NeighborSpace. Find out if there is an organization like this in your area, and if there is, try to work with them.

Potential Benefits of Working with a Community Garden Support Organization

➡ Established relationships with intercity organizations

➡ Processes for establishing communities and gardens

➡ Education programs

➡ Leadership and organizational training

➡ Liability insurance coverage

➡ Plant and seed distribution

➡ Access to free or low cost materials

If you are in a high-density urban area, land is often scarce; in suburban or rural areas, there may be plenty of land, but it might not be convenient for would-be gardeners to get to. Don't get me wrong, land is a good thing, and you have to work with what's available and where it's located. But it is important to remove as many obstacles as possible to get people involved early and enthusiastically, and if a garden is highly visible and convenient, it will be easier to attract participants. Plus, the aesthetic attributes of the garden will be a benefit to passersby. Some studies even indicate that the presence of a community garden can deter crime, such as in the case of the Tri-Neighborhood Community Garden in Norfolk, Virginia, mentioned earlier.

Types of Land

There are as many land scenarios as there are gardens, to be sure, but here are a few ways you can identify potential locations for the community garden.

Institutions Libraries, universities, hospitals, museums, police stations, schools, parks, and other organizations often have property available. These institutions may also have a mandate that aligns with your garden's mission, so you can help each other by putting in a community garden and bringing awareness to both of your organizations through increased usage or positive press.

What makes this scenario work? When underused resources gain more attention or traffic by being involved with community gardens, it benefits the institution that owns the property because they are beholden, either unofficially or officially as part of their charter, to serve the community. A community garden is a positive, visual reminder of an organization's commitments to its constituents.

Houses of worship It is not unusual to find unused land around religious institutions, and their mandate could line up with your garden's mission. In addition, they often have built-in communities that may need access to healthy, fresh food or may already work with food and nutrition programs in their areas.

What makes this scenario work? If your garden's mission is to grow food for those in need, working with a religious organization can be a slam-dunk relationship for both groups.

Businesses Particularly in the suburbs, there are corporate office parks with huge swaths of land ideal for community gardens. By partnering with a corporation, there is the potential to develop a garden that serves as a location for your community as well as a workplace garden for employees. There are also other types of businesses uniquely interested in community gardening, such as local nurseries, garden and building centers, and hardware stores.

What makes this scenario work? This is particularly beneficial if the corporation has health and wellness initiatives for its employees. For related retail businesses, having a community garden nearby or adjacent not only provides a built-in customer base but also serves as a living example of the usefulness of their products. The Peterson Garden Project established a partnership with a hardware store that provided free gloves on a weekly basis for our Volunteer of the Week program. The store also offered a 10 percent discount to any PGP gardeners who shopped there.

Private land If you've been eyeballing that empty, weedy lot in your neighborhood, chances are other people have, too. Chambers of commerce and local governments are usually aware of untended empty lots, so work with them to identify privately held property in your area. You can also go online and check tax records to identify ownership. In some cases, owners of untended lots can be fined by local governments if they are particularly weedy or unkempt. Your program could provide a benefit to the landowner by tending the property. Partnering to spruce up the neighborhood by way of a community garden can be mutually beneficial to all involved.

What makes this scenario work? In these cases, it is best to suggest a short-term garden. The landowner may have no immediate plans for the lot, but may want to sell or develop it in the future. In rare instances, you may be able to talk the owner into donating the property to your organization, but that takes time and relationship building. To swing this, you will most likely need 501c3 status. If your time frame to start a garden is fairly soon, a good solution is to make an agreement for a short duration, such as three to five years. Include an exit clause, so either party can terminate the agreement, with notice of an agreed-upon time period, with no hard feelings.

If the land you are using is for a defined time period, it is very important that your community understand and buy into the concept up front. People get very attached to their gardens, and without consensus on this approach, there could be hard feelings when the garden closes or moves at the end of the agreement. You can't overcommunicate this point to your gardeners. Plus, if your first garden

IS THE SOIL OKAY?

Soil contamination is a complex topic, and one that alarms a lot of people. While I strongly believe our gardens need to be healthy places, I also believe there can be an overemphasis on contamination that, in my opinion, scares people away from the natural world. If the site is just an average lot, there likely isn't much to worry about. And if you'll be using raised beds and trucking in soil, the risks are further reduced. The issue primarily applies to inground gardens where you'll be growing in existing soil. My opinion aside, here are the basics on soil toxins.

The two most common sources of contamination, lead-based paint and auto emissions, were regulated years ago, but harm to the soil is indeed ongoing. Environmental pollution in cities can also result in lead contamination of the soil, and metropolitan areas often have elevated lead levels—higher than those found naturally in agricultural regions. It is common knowledge that high concentrations of lead are toxic to humans, and exposure to lead by ingesting contaminated soil or dust is a danger.

Lead has the property of moving very little in soil, and it can be persistent over a long period of time. The highest concentrations of lead in urban settings occur most often in areas around building foundations and in proximity to busy streets. It is a continuing concern.

Though vegetable and fruit crops do not generally absorb or accumulate lead from soil, leafy vegetables such as lettuce can contain lead, and it may also be found in root crops, such as carrots. The risk of this contamination occurs on the surface of the plants rather than from the uptake within the plant.

Laws and regulations on remediating contaminated soil vary between regions and municipalities, and public and private lands, but mitigation is almost always expensive and time-consuming.

My advice is to use common sense when evaluating potential garden properties—a site that was once a chemical plant or a gas station is probably not a wise option (unless remediation has already occurred). You can also test the soil of any prospective property that you suspect might contain toxins; contact your local extension service or a similar agency and ask for assistance.

If for some reason you find yourself needing to pursue mitigation options, contact the agency in your area that governs such action.

---

ends with a mess of drama, future landowners might be less inclined to let you use their property. So frame the agreement in a positive light with your community, and make sure everyone enjoys and appreciates the property while they have it.

Municipal and county land Many cities and towns nationwide have, or are developing, programs where citizens can secure unused city property, for short- or long-term use, for purposes that benefits the community. Finding the agency to talk to in your city can be tricky, as the land could be owned or managed by a variety of entities—for example, the Department of Water (areas around bodies of water or rivers), Department of Transportation (rights-of-way near freeways, around bus stations, or similar), Department of Housing and Urban Development (land that is earmarked for use in long-term planning), and others. You really need to do your homework to determine the local government entity that oversees the property, and what permissions are needed for its use. Most cities have an office of urban planning, which is a good place to start. A different office will most likely work with you on the lease agreement for the property. Generally speaking, municipal land is relatively free or inexpensive to use. For technical reasons, a lease may require a minimal annual fee, which is sometimes as little as one dollar.

Working with a park district can be an easy path to identifying available land. Recreational and green space areas are often marked and easily identified, so it should be relatively simple to determine who needs to be contacted about potential land use. However, a park district's own mission may influence your intended garden in ways other city departments might not. For example, in Chicago, the park district has a mandate that there are to be no fences (except for security purposes near buildings or swimming pools), so all Chicago residents have equal access to all parks, at all times. This is a worthy goal. But if you want to grow food on park district land, you can't fence it, and theft becomes an issue. In New York City, parks allow fences, but community gardens must be open a certain number of hours per day so the public can enjoy them.

What makes this scenario work? Government organizations need to see the benefits of having community gardens on land in their control. Good press can often be a motivator for city organizations partnering with community groups. Many cities and municipalities are under pressure to create gardening programs, so your organization could help solve a burning issue on their to-do list.

Water

The next big challenge is water. There's no quicker way to kill a new garden (plants and community!) than to not have a viable water source worked out. And by viable, I mean easy for gardeners to use. Gardeners are generally willing to schlep water a bit within the garden itself, but are often not willing (at least not willing for long) to bring water with them or transport it from an inconvenient distance. This is very important! Don't let your enthusiasm for a garden outweigh this fundamental element. Here are some ways to establish a water source.

Ask the neighbors. The easiest way to get water is to ask the neighbors. Chances are, you're doing them a favor by cleaning up an unused piece of land, so they're often happy to help by offering a water source. It is easy to throw a hose over the fence to water a community garden, particularly if it is a small garden. If your neighbor has metered water (water they have to pay for), offer to chip in on the bill for the months the garden is active.

HOSES, TROUGHS, BUCKETS, AND CANS

Once you've got water into the garden, you need to think about how your gardeners will access it. Since water is something they will use frequently, maybe every day, it is often a big topic of conversation (and sometimes contention).

In an allotment garden, it is preferable to position the water source as centrally as possible, so everyone has easy access. If you have senior citizens or people with mobility issues, you may want to consider assigning them to beds as close to the water source as possible.

You also need to work through whether or not you will have hoses available for people to use, a water station where people can access a tap directly, whether there should be a reservoir like a horse trough where people can fill watering cans or buckets, or, if your budget allows, whether you should install an irrigation system. Most often seen in group-production row gardens, an irrigation system can be as simple as a series of soaker hoses or as complex as an elaborate network with timers. Most gardens can't afford an irrigation system, so don't stress out if you can't make this work within your budget.

There are challenges with all watering systems. If you use hoses, there's a chance that a gardener, while pulling the hose to his or her garden, may damage another person's plants. If you use a watering station, people may not return the watering cans or buckets (if you use shared ones) and a would-be waterer might have to go hunting for them. Another issue is making sure people turn the water off when they're done so there are no issues with running hoses and wasted resources. Be prepared: you will have to address situations around water throughout the season. It is important to train gardeners on best practices based on the watering system the garden has chosen. Don't be frustrated if this is an ongoing educational issue.

Tap a hydrant. A fire hydrant near your garden can be a godsend. Most cities have a department of water that is either an independent entity or part of another department such as streets and sanitation. Do a little digging to find out who's the boss when it comes to water. You will generally have to fill out an application to tap a hydrant. Depending on the hydrant, a special connector may be provided for you, or you may need to purchase one. This special connector will translate the fire-hose connection to a garden hose–size connection. If you have to purchase one, they can be pricey (up to $300). There may also be a fee to use the hydrant (to cover water costs). You'll find all this out when you talk to the person in charge of water.

Many hydrants are turned on with a key, which is a big iron wrench that turns a bolt on the hydrant to open the flow of water. You will need to decide whether to keep the water on at all times, or only have it on during specific hours. Whatever you decide, don't lose the key!

Hydrant situations usually work best when the hydrant is very close to the garden. You can run a hose across a sidewalk, but beware of any tripping danger you might be creating—make sure to tape down the hose or build a shallow, secured ramp to cover it, so nobody is hurt while passing by. If you run a hose across a street, protect the hose from traffic wear and tear. Using a protective speed bump sometimes requires another permit (from a different city department) as well as additional costs, so be sure to check into this first if you're considering stretching a hose across a street.

You will need to maintain the hose connection to the hydrant. Neighbors often get upset if water is leaking or spurting out of the hydrant. Permanently wet sidewalks and surrounding muddy or grassy areas aren't attractive and can be a hazard. If the hydrant is outside the perimeter (either fenced or unfenced) of your garden, there is also the chance that someone, out of malice, may slice your hose. It is a bummer, but it happens. Have a spare hose on hand just in case, and alert the police if this occurs.

Tap into an existing irrigation system. Particularly with institutions and corporate office parks, there may be an existing irrigation system you can tap into. Beware: working with a facility's maintenance people can be frustrating. Their job is primarily to keep up pristine lawns and landscapes—plants, shrubs, and trees. They may have opinions about the beauty (or value) of vegetable gardens. You'll have to work this out with the partners that control the property.

There are some costs to convert a sprinkler head to a water source. And there might be a system-wide timer that controls when you have access to water. None of these issues are insurmountable, but generally, the more issues to navigate, the slower (and sometimes more costly) the process can be.

Install a water source. If you are working with an established community garden support organization, they may have a process and available funds to install a tap in your community garden. Otherwise, your city officials might allow and even fund a dedicated water source.

Installing a water source isn't a difficult procedure, but it can be a difficult process. Some cities require an added, and costly, backflow protector. The logic is that if someone in your garden hooks up a sprayer to a hose (to distribute chemicals or other matter onto the garden), and if there is a fire down the block and firefighters tap the hydrant, the water use could create a backflow that would suction the water—and whatever chemicals being used—into the general water supply, contaminating the water. Of course, if you're gardening organically (and I hope you are), this shouldn't be an issue, but city rules might flatly require a backflow protector. If the issue comes up, you can state your case, but the rules may be the rules. Backflow protectors are not only expensive; they often require excavation to install.

Installing your own water source, preferably inside the garden, is a dream. Work with your city organizations to see if this is possible, but expect it to cost quite a bit, take some time, and involve haggling.

Use rain barrels. When discussing water for your community garden, the subject of rain barrels usually comes up. Depending on the size of your garden, proximity to a roof substantial enough to provide adequate runoff, and predictable rainfall, this scenario might work for you. There will be expenses to reroute the gutters from the building roof into the rain barrel or other capture mechanism, and there will be costs for the capture mechanism itself. If you are not near a building, it is possible to build capture structures out of plastic tarps. Plan on volunteer time to regularly clean and maintain the rain barrel or whatever capture system you use.

The rain-harvesting route can be a great experience for your community, as you reuse natural resources to keep your plants healthy. It can also be a great idea that doesn't get off the ground because of the cost or effort required for setup and maintenance. And it might not provide enough water for your garden, so be realistic when you consider this as an irrigation source. Perhaps it is a secondary source, in combination with other options.

Choosing Your Garden Type—Allotment, Group-Production, or Combo?

There's a lot of hairsplitting when it comes to defining a community garden. But by this point, having worked through the questionnaire and your mission statement, there have likely been discussions about how best to accomplish your mission within the garden. These discussions will help you decide whether your community garden should be an allotment or group-production type of arrangement.

The Allotment Garden

The term used for gardens built for individual or family use is "allotment," which means that gardeners are allotted a space to do with as they wish. There are usually some restrictions, though, on what can and cannot be done, which should be determined by the group when establishing the garden mission. For example, if the garden is organic, every gardener must adhere to the definition of organic gardening as decided on by the group.

Raised beds work well in allotment situations because the growing area is easily defined and recognized. If gardens are inground, participants are often allowed to define their allotted space with whatever barriers, fences, or decorations they wish. There might be turf wars in this scenario— gardeners have been known to try to horn in on their neighbor's plot, so be prepared.

The Group-Production Garden

When individuals come together to share the tasks of growing food that will either be distributed among the member gardeners or given away, it is called a group or production garden. Often gardens built in this format are interested in producing a large amount of food to fulfill their mission. Traditionally, raised beds aren't ideal for this type of garden, because it is easier to grow massive amounts with traditional row-farming methods.

The Combo Garden

Your garden could also have a combination of styles. While it's true that allotment gardeners generally do not want their produce taken by someone else, there are ways to accommodate both approaches. You might include an area where people garden together farm-style, to share produce with each other or the larger community, as well as an allotment area with raised beds where families grow and harvest food for their own use. And sharing isn't limited to production-style gardening. The community garden might also have raised beds for a shared herb garden, a seed-saving garden, a berry patch, or specific crops that are better suited to this type of growing.

There's no right or wrong way in your garden—but it *is* important to define and then communicate to all members the group's decision on the type of garden you'll be growing.

Soil

If your garden utilizes raised beds, the soil part of the equation is fairly simple. One of the advantages is that contamination is not a problem, because you will be bringing in soil rather than using what's existing at the site. Find either a landscape contractor or wholesaler who will source and deliver the soil to the garden. Then you will need to get the soil from the pile dumped by the truck into the raised beds; this is a good project for the gardeners. Particularly in an allotment scenario, gardeners will hopefully be eager to make their part of the community garden happen. Plus, it is good for the gardeners to provide sweat equity in the building of the garden. Don't be shy about asking them to fill their own raised beds, and assigning other tasks to non-gardening volunteers.

Inground Growing

Presuming that your existing soil does not contain toxins, if you're planning a group-production garden with inground rows, you'll still need to address the quality of the soil. While it may not be contaminated, the soil may not be particularly fertile. There are entire books on soil health; but the easiest way to judge what you have to work with is by having the soil tested to assess fertility levels (again, your local extension service or similar organization are good resources).

If your soil needs amendments to increase fertility, it will take money, resources, and equipment. Maybe you'll require compost to boost fertility, sand to improve drainage, or some other supplement. Then you'll need a way to spread these materials and integrate them into the soil. Volunteers love these types of projects; just make sure there are enough volunteers to accommodate the size of your garden. If not, you might want to consider augmenting the soil by working with a landscape company that has heavy equipment.

To Compost or Not to Compost

Compost is a valuable component in healthy soil, and as you enter years two and three of your garden, soil health will be an important issue your team will have to address. In your first year— starting with your new, healthy soil—you should be good to go, and few or no further soil amendments will be required. But I promise you, one of the first things someone will ask in your community meetings is "Will there be composting?" This is a question you need to consider very carefully.

Composting is a blanket term that can be confusing. Many people think of compost as kitchen food scraps (banana peels, eggshells, unused bits of vegetables, and even coffee grounds or paper towels). However, your garden will generate a lot of spent plant material—pruned leaves, rotten vegetables, removed plants that have bolted (gone to flower or seed premature) or are dead at the end of the season—and these can all be composted, as well.

Composting is a relatively simple process—time and heat convert these materials to useful garden matter. But managing a compost program in a community garden is not so simple. First, you need a few volunteers dedicated to managing the program: tending the piles, turning them, adding materials when needed and available. And in a community garden, you need to educate your gardeners constantly on what can and cannot be put in a compost pile. Not all food scraps and not all spent plant matter can be composted. Meat, fish, and cooked food are no-nos, for example, as are weeds that have gone to seed and diseased plants. This education and monitoring can be an ongoing, frustrating endeavor.

SOIL FROM LANDSCAPE CONTRACTORS: THINGS TO KNOW

Acquiring soil for a community garden is a bigger endeavor than getting soil for a backyard. Instead of going to a nursery or big-box store and getting a few bags of soil, you'll order in quantity, by the cubic yard. A raised bed that is 4 ft. by 8 ft. by 8 in. takes almost one cubic yard. If you have ninety raised beds, you can visualize how much soil is required for a community garden. But no need to panic! There are professionals out there who can help you. They specialize in bulk soil orders and, by following these tips, you'll know the right questions to ask to make sure everything goes smoothly.

➡ If you know nothing about soil, find someone who does, or educate yourself before you talk to a landscape contractor or wholesaler.

➡ Have a rough idea of the soil mixes you want to use (usually a mix of composts, topsoil, and other elements such as sand or peat).

➡ Find a landscape contractor or wholesaler who understands vegetable gardening vs. landscape gardening. Ask for a few references from vegetable or community gardeners who have worked with a landscaper and call them to make sure the soil they received worked well.

➡ If you are relying on the contractor's or wholesaler's expertise, be clear about the type of soil you want and communicating the intended use (vegetable gardening). Ask their expertise for what will work best within your budget.

➡ Understand how much soil mix you will need. Explain your garden scenario and ask the landscape contractor to calculate the cubic yards required. This will affect price and delivery.

➡ Be prepared to pay a bit more for organic soil mixes.

➡ Ask them to view the garden entry before they deliver— there may be obstacles (telephone wires, gate size, impossible turn radius) that prevent them from using a certain dump truck size.

➡ Be there during delivery to ensure you get what you ordered. If a delivery doesn't look right, speak up immediately.

➡ The soil supplier may not be able to deliver in rainy weather. Develop a back-up delivery plan.

➡ If rain is expected on the day of delivery, request help to cover and secure the soil with tarps. (You will want to keep your soil as dry as possible. It is hard to shovel mud—plus, wet soil compacts into a less-than-perfect growing medium.)

If you have a short-term lease on your garden space, the effort and space required might not be worth it. If you have secured garden land for a longer period, consider getting the garden started for a year or two to understand your gardeners' and volunteers' level of dedication before committing to a compost program.

Here are a couple of options if you don't want to manage a composting program in the community garden.

➡ Work with a local composting program to use your garden space as a pickup site. Some food scrap programs provide five-gallon buckets to homeowners to fill with kitchen scraps. The full buckets are then traded out for empty buckets. This exchange could happen in your garden and you could work with the compost program to have the garden buy the compost made from the scraps (or have it donated to the garden).

➡ Landscapers are often willing to pick up big quantities of spent plant matter to add to their own compost program or to drop off with a partner. In Chicago, we work with a local landscaper at the beginning and end of the season to provide giant sacks. We instruct our gardeners to put spent plant material in the sacks, and, when they are full, our landscape partner comes and gets them. I have to tell you, though, as much as we tell people "no trash," it always finds its way into the sacks. Glass, rocks, and other non-compostable items are frustrating for the landscapers and composters and, at some point, they may stop accepting the garden's plant material because of this.

This is the type of monitoring and education I'm talking about. If you have the ability to talk with gardeners frequently, one-on-one, about protocol around these types of programs, success is greater than if you have a lot of people reading signage or e-mail messages (or not reading at all).

The consequences of a poorly managed compost system include odors and insects. And the neighbors are not going to like that at all. If you don't have neighbors, this might not be a problem, but if you are in a dense urban area, you must keep the neighbors happy at all costs.

Don't feel guilty if you decide not to have a compost program. Successful composting requires time, energy, and a level of commitment that some groups just may not be able to provide. Better to assess your organization's level of dedication to the necessary education and maintenance before you start a compost program than to find out too late that it's not workable.

Wood Chips

Wood chips are to gardens what paint is to redecorating—they both cover a lot of sins. Wood chips are often as important to a garden as soil, but for different reasons.

Many city forestry departments have an excess of wood chips from maintaining forests and urban trees. Your garden could be a good partner for a forestry department with a lot of excess chips. Oftentimes they are free and sometimes you can request a certain grade; the terms are generally "rough chips," which are sent one time through the shredder, and "fine chips," which have been through two or more times.

The likelihood of being able to enlist volunteers to shovel and move wood chips really depends on the size of your garden, the involvement of the members, and the number of people available. Another option is to work with someone who has a front-end loader, or to rent one (you will have no trouble finding a volunteer who wants to drive it, I promise), or to hire someone with the right machinery to spread the chips for you. You can also engage a landscape contractor. If you are part of a citywide community gardening organization, chances are they will have resources you can tap into as well.

Garden Supplies and Amenities

When it comes to supply needs for the garden, consider the items for one-time or occasional use (lots of shovels and wheelbarrows to move all that soil and all those wood chips), and items for ongoing use (hoses, watering cans, and garden tools). Decide what the garden as an organization will provide, what the gardeners need to provide for themselves, and what can be borrowed from local organizations for special projects or group activities.

Garden supplies are a great way to get participants involved in constructing the garden. Many people have extra wheelbarrows and shovels that get used infrequently (and may be taking up space). After compiling your wish list, ask volunteers to donate tools and other supplies on a short-term, long-term, or permanent basis. If items are on loan, and the gardeners want their stuff back at some point, make them responsible for marking items clearly with their name, in a way that will last all season (masking tape with a name written with a waterproof pen might be enough, or something more substantial may be required). If members donate other materials as a gift to the garden, be sure to thank them publicly and let everyone know what they donated. This will not only make the donor feel good, but will provide a good example for other gardeners to pitch in as well.

If you can't get all the equipment you need from your gardeners — particularly for one-time projects—often neighborhood parks have extra shovels and wheelbarrows they may allow you to borrow for a few days. It doesn't hurt to make friends with your local parks department! They might also have horticultural experts on staff who can provide advice or education for you or your gardeners.

Besides supplies, there are other amenities you may want to consider for your garden. Your community might be thinking a storage shed would be awfully nice. Maybe some benches and—oh! A pergola for shade! And maybe a stage! It is easy to be a dreamer in the garden.

THE ABSOLUTE BASIC GARDEN SUPPLY LIST

➡ Hand tools
➡ Hoes
➡ Hoses
➡ Rakes
➡ Shovels
➡ Watering cans

➡ Grill and cooking area (if your lease
agreement allows for fire on-site)

➡ Picnic benches and tables

➡ Children's play area

➡ Pergolas, gazebos, or other
decorative structures (better for
gardens where you have a long
tenure)

➡ Greenhouses or hoop houses for
season extension

➡ Beehives (better for gardens
without a lot of small children)

➡ Stage or performance area

Before you know it, your imaginary garden has an outdoor kitchen, a built-in sound system, and a hot tub. Some stuff is necessary and some stuff is nice to have. Remember, you don't need to do everything the first year. (And after you've shoveled all those wood chips and soil, that advice will make even more sense.)

Start with a storage area. This can be as simple as a plastic storage chest from a big-box home store, or as elaborate as a custom-built toolshed. For the first year, start out with something simple and practical, such as a lockable storage chest. Once you understand your garden community's needs and the skill sets of your volunteer base, then decide on the best method to store equipment. And remember, if you're building any permanent structures in the garden, research permit requirements before you start.

Seating is nice, particularly if you have older gardeners. This can be as uncomplicated as lawn chairs, or as fancy as park benches. If you have a shady spot, that's a natural place for seating. Again, start out with the bare necessities your first year and build from there.

Security: On the Fence

This is a hot topic and there's no right answer. If you don't fence your community food garden, there will be theft issues, I promise you. If you do fence, you will be criticized for keeping the community out. I'm warning about this now so you can prepare yourself. People get funny where food access is involved, particularly on city-owned or other communal property.

If your garden's mission is to provide food for local food and nutrition programs, then the no-fence option may be the way to go. You might not be delivering the food in the manner you had thought, but it will go to the community.

If people are growing for their families in an allotment garden or you are teaching people to garden, you might want to have a fence. It is a real bummer to lose that prize tomato or watermelon that your beginning gardener has been nurturing all summer. In a suburban or rural area, there might be surprising thieves, such as deer. Consider the community, the garden's mission, and the budget, and decide accordingly.

At least in urban areas, empty lots are often required to be fenced for safety purposes. These fences are generally inexpensive construction fences and aren't a hundred percent secure. But this type of temporary fencing is enough for property owners to signify the land is private and fulfill obligations to the city. So, when you get your land, there might already be a fence if the city requires one, which is great. If you don't have a fence, and you want one, they are costly (even the cheapo temporary construction fences). Do some research to determine costs and budget accordingly.

If you have a fence and want to lock the gate, there are some decisions to make. You'd think something as simple as a lock would be, well, simple. It's not. Do you post open hours and designate a person who is responsible for unlocking and locking the gate on a regular schedule? Or do you allow gardeners to come and go as they please? If you allow them to come and go as they please, you will either have to provide keys or the code to a combination lock. These options can present problems: lost keys, people unable to open the lock because of forgotten codes; an unreliable, regularly scheduled gate opener. Inevitably there will be complications with locking your garden. Think through the choices and set up a reliable system at the beginning—and remain good-natured when you get your third call in one day about the lock not working.

Tricks to Deter Theft

If your mission includes providing a completely open garden where any and all can help themselves, ignore the following advice. But if you can't afford or don't want a fence for mission-driven reasons, you will have to come up with ways to thwart sticky fingers. Here are a few ideas.

➡ Around the perimeter of the garden, plant a series of beds in which the food grown is available to the public. Indicate this area with signage, so people know the produce is available for the taking; consider additional signage for plots that are not for public harvesting. With this strategy, you can also provide educational information on how to pick produce, or how to tell when it is ripe.

➡ Use visual (non-fence) separators such as plastic flags or rope to identify the off-limits areas of your garden. Signage can be used to share your logic with guest harvesters.

➡ Plant things people don't recognize! White eggplants, white or green-when-ripe tomatoes, purple peppers, golden watermelons, and oddly colored or variegated herbs make people think twice about picking something they don't immediately recognize.

➡ If your program is dedicated to growing food for food pantries, nutrition programs, or some other worthy cause, let people know; create signage that explains the public service the garden is providing. This can reduce unauthorized harvesting.

THIEVING DEER: A FUNNY STORY

I was once visiting a community garden and struck up a conversation with one of the organizers. We were chatting about various community garden management issues, when the topic of fences came up. She mentioned that they had recently given up and put up a fence because the gardeners were so discouraged by all the losses. I sympathized with her and nodded in agreement as I listened to her tale. After a few minutes, We both sighed and I said, "Thieves!" as she simultaneously said, "Deer!" It was a funny moment because in our urban gardens, people are the culprits. In her suburban site, deer are the offenders. We'd talked about fences for almost five minutes, thinking we were talking about the same issue! We both got a good laugh out of it—and learned that for all of the similarities in our city and country community gardens, there are differences as well!

Neighbor Concerns

In addition to the compost issues discussed earlier, there are other worries your neighbors may have as your garden starts to take shape. You'll probably hear these objections at your early community meetings. If they don't come up then, great. But don't be surprised if they surface later, once the garden is established.

Bad odors Rightly or wrongly, people think big gardens are stinky. Probably because they haven't been around gardens much. But all that talk of fertilizer and compost gets some neighbors nervous. Most garden products aren't smelly, so, practically speaking, this isn't a real issue. But managing *perceptions* is sometimes more challenging than managing reality.

Insects Similar to bad odors, people worry about flies and other unwanted pests being attracted to a garden. This comes up when people inquire about compost programs, too. Unless you get a biblical plague of locusts, this shouldn't be an issue, but, again, perception is everything.

Vermin This term covers a lot of pests. But mostly, people are afraid of rats. And rightly so—they carry disease and are creepy. The way to keep rats away is make sure there is nowhere for them to hide and nothing for them to eat or drink. As scary as they are, rats are timid creatures for the most part, and won't come around when people are in the garden. (I did once see a brazen city rat sashaying down the middle aisle of a movie theater.) They are also mostly nocturnal and have poor eyesight.

A perfect scenario for rats is a garden with lots of overhang on the edges of beds and the garden's perimeter, which provides places to hide and access to food (such as vegetables lying on the ground—rats are attracted to the smell of rotting vegetables or very fragrant fruits like melons). Since they have poor eyesight, they follow corners and walls using their whiskers to help them navigate. So if the rat superhighways around your garden are covered with vegetation, you're just encouraging them. They also need water, so try to minimize standing water in puddles or ponds (raccoons are also attracted to ponds). A tidy, well-harvested and dry garden will be an unfriendly place to rats—but a friendly, safe place to humans and neighbors, which brings me to the next item.

SMALL BEDS, FREE CHIPS, AND FENCES: THE PETERSON GARDEN PROJECT

My home community garden is the Peterson Garden Project, which I started with no partners or outside funding. The community members funded the building of the garden and, after the first year, added additional programs. This meant the materials used were very basic (untreated pine boards and free chips from the city). The property was fenced (due to city requirements), which worked out well for two reasons: it was on a busy intersection and it discouraged theft. This latter benefit was especially important, since the mandate of the garden was to teach, and it seemed that community members would be much more likely to become lifelong gardeners if their amateur attempts weren't foiled by having the fruits of their labors go missing.

The educational mandate also affected the build of the garden. The organizers removed as much complexity as possible for gardeners to join. Beds were a small, predetermined size (4 ft. by 8 ft., so as to not overwhelm new gardeners), all plots were the same size to make instruction simple, and organic methods were employed and practiced (this determined the kind of soil we brought in and how gardeners were taught). Community areas were included in the building plan—a seating area and also a stage—to support the social aspect of the garden.

Removing complexity was also tied to the history of the garden. The site was an original World War II victory garden. During the war, 90 percent of the food gardeners in the city had never gardened before, so we actively recruited people who had little or no gardening experience. The simple, uniform space was a great help for this new crop of gardeners.

Now, with the project entering its fifth year, many of the original participants have mastered the basic gardening techniques taught at Peterson gardens, and have gone on to be leaders and educators in new gardens.

The original land agreement was short-term. We knew the physical garden would only last as long as the property was available, so the small beds, stage, and other areas were built to be easily moved. Everything was made to be portable so the garden could move to new, unused land.

To date, Peterson Garden Project has moved three gardens to new locations and built a total of eleven. The community moves with the gardens and, each spring when fresh gardens are created, new people learn the basic tasks of food growing, community, and garden building.

Untidiness When you say "garden," most people think ornamental beds that are grown for their beauty. Vegetable gardens, while beautiful in their own right, are grown to produce food. And, at certain times of the year, they can look a little unkempt. As a vegetable gardener, you might not mind beans drying on the vine, but the neighbors might see them as a bunch of dead plants. It is important to consider the aesthetics of the community garden, particularly in areas visible to neighbors or passersby. If you don't hear this as a concern before you start your garden, you will once the garden is in. Be prepared to address these issues and respect that not everyone appreciates the unique attributes of a vegetable garden or even cares. Plan accordingly. Often some delicious homegrown tomatoes delivered with a smile are all it takes to soothe a ruffled neighbor.

THIRD MEETING: DESIGNING THE GARDEN

So far, there has been a lot of information presented. Some of it might apply to your project, some might not. Don't be overwhelmed or think you have to incorporate it all, or that you must set up your garden to match the gardens that were presented earlier in the case studies. Those gardens have evolved to suit their communities' needs. Now it's time to create *your* unique garden! In this third community meeting, members and participants will have a chance to determine what the garden will be like. This is going to be fun!

Design Considerations

As pencils meet sketch pads (or whatever people are using to convey their dream garden), the realities of what goes into a community garden will start to pop up. Keep visions grounded in practicality by reminding participants of important design factors.

Paths These should be, at a minimum, 3 feet wide. If any partnering organizations require Americans with Disabilities Act (ADA) compliance, make sure you know what those requirements are and how they might impact your budget.

Raised beds If your garden is going to have raised beds, they shouldn't be too wide (gardeners shouldn't be stepping in the soil). Make sure they are no more than 4 feet wide, so all crops can be accessed easily around the perimeter of the bed. If you need to situate gardens against a fence, put the short ends against the fence (chain link makes a great trellis). If you must put a raised bed longwise against a fence, make it no deeper than 3 feet so a gardener can reach across from the side opposite the fence.

Water Consider the garden water source. Depending on the watering method you want to use—watering stations or hoses—make sure to leave room around the watering area. Watering areas tend to be wet, and nearby gardeners might have to deal with soggy conditions, or kids playing with water. Provide a little distance so everyone stays happy.

Sun For a vegetable garden, you need six to eight hours of direct sun for popular crops like tomatoes, peppers, and eggplants to grow. Some crops, like leafy greens, can handle partial or dappled shade. Keep these factors in mind as you're designing your garden to make sure that, in an allotment situation, everyone has enough light to grow; and in a group-production garden, specific beds can be set up for crops with different light requirements. You don't have to get into

DREAM GARDENS
Agenda for the Third Community Meeting

By now, with two community meetings under your belt, you and your team are getting used to the format. Knowing your group, you will need to determine if this next step will require one or more meetings. There's a lot of important community work here—you want people as involved as possible, but you also don't want to burn them out with too many meetings. Only you know the commitment level of your group, and how much time you have to go through a complete design process. As leaders, you may have to make some judgment calls about how much group involvement there can be to move things forward.

⇒ WELCOME

Introduce yourself once again, as well as any teammates or special guests who are leading the meeting. Thank people for attending.

⇒ OVERVIEW

Briefly state the purpose of the meeting: you're going to start the design process for the garden! You may want to reiterate the hard work you've done to date, including developing your mission statement. Be sure to comment about your previous meetings and how everyone has gotten to this place *together*. Either recite the mission statement or write it on a big flip chart for everyone to see. This design exercise is the time when you'll need it most!

⇒ GROUND RULES

Discuss meeting length, how off-topic comments will be handled, and any other information about group participation. Continue to reinforce the group norms that are developing. Depending on how much time you have, you may want to revisit the Attributes of a Successful Group list, and make sure everyone feels you are moving in the right direction as a group.

⇒ AGENDA REVIEW

Hopefully, everyone is aware of why they're meeting—this can be solidified via the agenda review. Let people add extra items or discuss outstanding issues from the last meeting, if they are important to someone.

⇒ INTRODUCTIONS

If the group composition is similar to the first meeting, have everyone quickly restate their name and the organization they represent (if any). If there are new participants, ask them to introduce themselves and, if applicable, their organization, and to give a brief overview of their interest in the garden.

⇒ ACTION ITEM(S)

The action item for this meeting is a two-part design charrette. You can either explain the charrette process to the group, or distribute a handout with a description of the process, or both.

Charrette (pronounced *shuh-ret*) is French for "chariot," and refers to a process in which a group designs or creates something collaboratively. Using this process, it can take several meetings to come to consensus. The heart of the idea is that small groups work on an element of the design and present it to the bigger group. A successful charrette promotes joint ownership of solutions, and attempts to diffuse confrontational attitudes that often arise when community assets are involved—in this case, shared garden space.

The process begins by organizing a visioning exercise with your community. Each of your gardeners and participants will have a chance to present an image of their ideal garden, after which the community as a whole can get down to brass tacks and make a plan for the garden—one that, hopefully, incorporates some part of everyone's dreams!

RECAP

This was hard work! Congratulate everyone on their efforts. Encourage people to share comments and talk about how this process made them feel.

NEXT STEPS

These will depend on where you wound up in your design process. You might be done with the design phase after this meeting, you might need to have other meetings, or you might need to have a subgroup or a professional take the best elements of a few consensus-driven designs and incorporate those elements into one master design. Only you will know the best approach at this juncture.

CALENDAR

Find a time for the next meeting or reiterate a predetermined date.

WRAP-UP

This is heavy-duty work. Chances are, people are tired. Recognize the work the group accomplished. If it was tough, bring that up (never shy away from acknowledging what some might consider a challenging experience). If it was joyous, bring that up. Whatever vibe happened during this time, bring it up. This is also a good time to look to the future. Sure, you may all be planning in a church basement in the dead of winter but in three, six, or twelve months, the garden that you collectively dreamed up will be an asset to the community. This is exciting stuff! And, as always, a heartfelt thank-you is in order. And, maybe, hugs all around!

HANG OUT

If you're not all exhausted and ready to get away from each other or go home and collapse, consider a decompression drink at a local gathering place. Or just hang for a few minutes, clean up, and see if anyone has any comments.

DESIGN CHARRETTE BREAKOUT

Designing the garden in this exercise isn't about reality—you want to get to rough concepts here; renderings of how the garden space might make community members feel. Encourage people to use words that represent the attributes they may be drawing. Words like *play, safe, joy, bountiful,* and *healthy* are words that may pop up. And let people know this isn't about their drawing skills or ability. Think of it like a child's drawing—evocative of feelings but not based on things like bed dimensions or the actual garden space. We'll get to practical issues in the next part of the exercise; this first part is about dreams.

PART 1: DREAM GARDENS—VISIONING

Have attendees break into small groups. As always, group sizes depend on the number of attendees; six to eight people per group, generally. Give the groups 20 to 30 minutes to complete this exercise.

Participants will need 11-by-17-inch sheets of paper and lots of colored markers. Allow 10 to 15 minutes for each participant to draw her or his dream garden. After that, allow 10 to 15 minutes for everyone to share their dream gardens within the small group. Have one person in each group take notes or write on a big flip chart the words or themes that emerge from this exercise (these will be reported back to the larger group). If your space allows, put all the drawings on the wall and allow time for the larger group to review all the drawings.

This exercise serves multiple purposes. It gets the participants thinking creatively and it reinforces that everyone's ideas are valuable. It also reinforces that gardens are more than the mechanics of the number of beds or where the water is located; it emphasizes that gardens are places where people are connected emotionally. Finally, it visually reminds all participants that everyone thinks differently and has different hopes and dreams for the garden. You've heard the saying, "A picture is worth a thousand words." This exercise cuts through all the discussion and gets to the heart of what people are trying to describe when they talk about the garden. That's why it is important to post and share everyone's dream garden and allow time for review if possible. It isn't that one or two gardens might be the basis for the next step (although they might be); it is to illustrate that there are many ways of thinking and many visions of what the garden can mean to people once it is constructed. This exercise will provide a lot of meaningful "ah-ha" moments.

PART 2: GARDEN GIVENS—THE LAYOUT

At this time in your community process, you will likely have made some critical observations: the size of the garden; how it is oriented; where and when the sun hits; where there are existing trees, buildings, or other features that will impact layout; where the water is coming from; entrances; whether or not a fence exists.

In the second step of this exercise, you'll use a rough drawing showing the basic space with the givens indicated. Now the groups will begin translating their dream gardens into a communal space.

Prior to the meeting, someone needs to produce a rough framework drawing of the space, with the garden givens, that can be photocopied onto 11-by-17-inch paper. Don't stress about accuracy too much, but try to make the framework drawing relatively true in terms of space. Using graph paper can help. Indicate the givens on the drawing, but keep things as conceptual as possible so attendees don't think that someone else has done all the designing. Hand these basic drawings out at the meeting.

Have attendees return to their small groups. Ask each participant to spend 10 minutes drawing a rough translation of their dream garden on top of the foundation template. Have members take into account the garden mission, the designated givens, as well as other design considerations. Then, provide extra blank foundation garden drawings and ask participants to combine all of the group's

visions into one final drawing, using pencils or colored markers. Give each group 30 to 45 minutes to complete this exercise.

Reconvene into a large group and allow 10 minutes for everyone to share the dream gardens within the small group.

This exercise might or might not be easy. This is where all the community building that has been done to date—for example, creating group norms about respecting opinions and ideas; the shared vision of the mission statement—start to (hopefully) reap rewards. You'll also see certain individuals rise up through this discussion by either moderating or using their drawing skills (or both) to get the group's collective garden on paper. There might be struggles or disagreements. There might be laughter or raised voices. This is all welcome, and exactly the point of this exercise—to get people designing together, creating together, coming to agreement together.

If you have many groups, put individual group drafts on a wall and take 10 minutes for everyone to review all the different versions. You'll start to see themes emerge! If you have just a few small groups, go ahead and have each group present their findings without posting the images on a wall. Hopefully you'll find consistent ideas showing up in multiple garden designs that the groups presented

You have a few choices at this point—you can press on and combine elements from the individual gardens into one collective group design, with one appointed person using a blank handout to incorporate elements from all of the groups' drawings. Or, if, after this exercise, people are a bit fried, go ahead and end the meeting (on a positive note) and agree to return for more refining at the next meeting. You can also agree to turn the ideas over to a landscape designer or artist volunteer from your group to compile the ideas into a narrower selection of one to three design concepts, which can be presented and voted on when the drawings are presented at your next gathering.

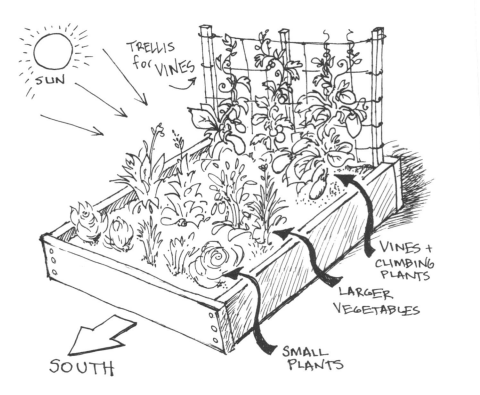

SUN

TRELLIS for VINES

VINES + CLIMBING PLANTS

LARGER VEGETABLES

SMALL PLANTS

SOUTH

Plan for sun and shading when you plant.

the nitty-gritty of this now (light needs for specific crops will be covered in chapter 7), but be aware of how sunlight will impact growing conditions for all the gardeners and their plots.

Gate If the garden is to have a fence, account for the swing radius of the gate in your design when placing raised beds or garden rows. If the gate is located on an alley or street, make sure it swings inward so car or pedestrian traffic can't become blocked.

Clearance Amenities like benches, storage areas and containers, compost bins, and stages need easy access and clearance space. Shared amenities are best situated, when possible, where most gardeners can reach them easily.

Accessibility You may have senior citizens or people with mobility issues as members. Accessibility needs to be well thought out. To make gardening as simple as possible for these participants, consider positioning their areas or raised beds as close to the entrance and amenities as possible. Some seating nearby is nice, too.

Communication station Set aside a highly visible area for communicating with gardeners, such as a sheltered whiteboard or corkboard.

Place it where organizational and personal messages and announcements can easily be posted by and for the gardeners.

MAKING IT REAL

Once you get to consensus and choose a preliminary design, congratulate yourselves! At this point the community garden members, leaders, and even those who have yet to commit, will likely be able to see that a shared vision has evolved out of all the hard work and cooperation.

By this time in the process, you'll hopefully have identified some garden experts in your community. They could be Master Gardeners, landscape designers, knowledgeable enthusiasts, or people who have worked at local nurseries. If nobody in your community has experience with building a garden, you might need to seek out someone to help draft plans or, at least, to review them before building begins.

The next stage, following the preliminary design development, is to do some research on costs for the different elements dreamed up for the new community garden. This process doesn't have to be driven by the group—a few eager volunteers can do some calling around to price out the features. These numbers will be the basis for your budget. Once the budget numbers come together, you'll begin to see where fiscal reality comes into play in the garden. If your dreams far outstrip your funding, or the amount of energy your gardeners can contribute to the garden, then it is time to talk phases.

An easy way to launch phasing is to set up a basic garden infrastructure on the site: build garden beds, establish the soil and water supplies, and decide on any other basic essentials that will get the organization up and running. Other desired amenities—an entertainment stage or pergola, for instance—can be left to a second phase. Perhaps that next phase occurs during the winter—a nice opportunity for garden members to continue working together through the cold, non-growing months.

The point is, don't give up just because you can't do everything at once. Members will feel much better with a few small successes rather than lots of big projects that don't get done. The bonus to this approach is that once the community gets through a full season of growing together, ideas that were originally considered essential may become less necessary to the community's evolving vision and needs. And since you want the garden to be around for the long haul, there is plenty of time to add features as the seasons come and go. Time will also help everyone understand how fiscal demands and dreams interact.

THE RAISED BED
Materials and Construction

If your community garden is like many, it will employ raised beds, and that means learning how to build them! Before you or anyone associated with your garden builds anything, however, you will need to establish safety protocols for your garden organization, which are discussed in chapters 4 and 5. Make sure every person engaged in any activity in the garden has signed the appropriate waivers, and understands the safety rules you have set forth.

Raised beds are generally made of new, untreated wood, but bricks and cinder blocks or recycled wood can work, too. If your garden is small, you might consider working with a rebuilding exchange to procure materials. Just make sure that the recycled materials you use are free of chemicals. This is particularly important with lumber.

Your budget will dictate the type of wood you can purchase. Pine is less expensive, but doesn't last as long as other woods. Cedar and redwood last many years, but are more expensive. Really, any type of wood will work for a raised bed, just make sure it is untreated. Treated lumber will be the majority of what you'll find at lumber suppliers because it has many commercial uses. Chemicals are applied to the wood to make it fire retardant, to slow the natural process of decay, and to prevent termites and other insects from inflicting damage. Railroad ties, which come in convenient sizes, are generally treated with creosote, another toxic chemical. These treatments give the wood durability for use in fences, homes, and other buildings—but the chemicals can leach into the soil (and things growing in that soil), making treated wood a poor choice for vegetable garden beds. Don't take chances—ask specifically for untreated wood.

The beds are fairly simple to construct, even for volunteers. Buying the lumber will be a big expense for your garden, but purchasing in quantity may qualify you for a discount. Also, be sure to tell your supplier that you are a community garden and ask for any discounts they may offer for all your needed materials. There are many places to purchase wood, including lumberyards, big-box stores, and local hardware stores. Shop around and see who will give you the best price. You might also want to negotiate a sponsorship in exchange for greatly reduced pricing or even free goods.

Obviously, one of the key factors in building your raised beds is just how big they're going to be. Generally speaking, 8 feet is a good length. Lumber comes in 8- and 10-foot lengths and can be cut by the lumber supplier, usually free of charge. Regarding the width of the bed, make sure it is no wider than 4 feet, or 3 feet if it is going to be situated against a wall or fence. This way the gardeners can reach in comfortably from the outside without having to step on the soil.

To build a basic wood frame, you'll need four 2-by-6-inch boards, cut to the desired length. If you want the sides to be higher, you'll work with 8-, 10-, or 12-inch boards. And if you want them to be thicker, that's fine, too; 2-inch boards are a starting point because they're easy to work with, as well as economical.

Additional materials you'll need include corner posts (standard size is 4 by 4 inches), deck screws (twice as long as the lumber thickness, to ensure a secure fit; so, for a 2-inch board, use 4-inch screws), and a power drill. If you wish to deter weeds or are bringing in soil and don't want to have it mix with the garden soil that's beneath the bed, you will also need a barrier the dimensions of your bed, for the bed to rest on.

If you're using materials other than wood, such as concrete blocks or bricks, the construction process is straightforward: line them up and stack them straight. Each bed's walls should be at least 6 inches high to contain the soil and provide enough room for plants to grow. Beds can be built taller, regardless of materials—just be prepared to fill them with more soil. Taller raised beds (24 inches or higher) are a nice perk for some of the senior gardeners in your community. Their knees will appreciate the thoughtful planning and kind gesture. Just remember: more soil equals higher cost.

ASSEMBLY INSTRUCTIONS FOR RAISED BEDS

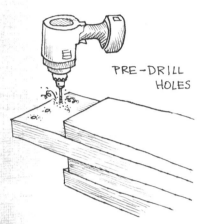

PRE-DRILL HOLES

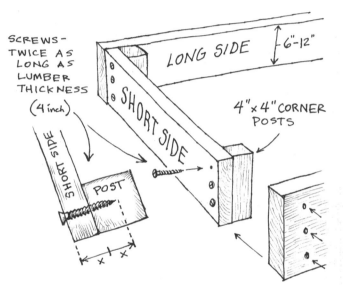

2" × 6"-12" UNTREATED LUMBER

LONG SIDE

6"-12"

SCREWS—TWICE AS LONG AS LUMBER THICKNESS (4 inch)

SHORT SIDE

SHORT SIDE

POST

4" × 4" CORNER POSTS

x   x

1. Using a drill bit that's a little smaller in diameter than your screws, pre-drill 2 to 3 holes into the end of each board (this helps prevent the wood from splitting when you drive in the screws). Have a board or two underneath the one being drilled to keep the drill bit from hitting the ground when it pokes through the wood.

2. Put together the short sides of the frame first. Position the end of the board against a corner post and screw the pieces together. Screw a second corner post into the opposite end. Repeat for the other short side. Attach the long sides of the frame to the short sides.

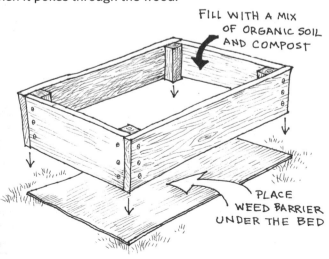

FILL WITH A MIX OF ORGANIC SOIL AND COMPOST

PLACE WEED BARRIER UNDER THE BED

3. If applicable, place a barrier beneath the bed frame. Fill the bed with your soil mix.

4. TAKING CARE OF GARDEN BUSINESS

A Structure for Sustainability

For years, neighbors have been guerrilla gardening on empty lots, growing food and community with very little formal organization, legal structure, or even rules. While the simplest approach is usually the best, there will be situations in which it will be necessary to create a formal structure for your garden, with all the legalities that kind of structure entails. Legal matters and accounting may not be as much fun as gardening and building community, but they are vital to the long-term success of the organization and the garden community it represents.

If your group has the opportunity to be, or is already, part of a larger organization, much of the information in this section will be addressed by your parent organization. For those of you starting new organizations, there are key elements you will need to consider to manage the business side of things. Set these components up the right way at the start, and they will be woven into the fabric of operations, so nobody has to worry about them in the future.

NONPROFIT STATUS

Many garden organizations eventually have the "Should we be a nonprofit organization?" talk—and for good reason. Nonprofit status can provide a lot of benefits.

In the United States, federal recognition as a nonprofit 501c3 organization is a two-step process: action at both the state and federal level is required. The first step involves being recognized by your state. This type of status is usually helpful when seeking funding on a local level, but it does not provide tax-exempt status—the garden organization will have to pay state sales taxes as well as state and federal income taxes. To have your garden recognized on the state level, you can file

> *Opportunity is missed by most people because it is dressed in overalls and looks like work.*
>
> —Thomas Edison

85

as a nonprofit or a for-profit organization, although most community garden organizations are nonprofit because they don't, generally, have a profit-driven motive. (For-profits are not eligible to apply for federal 501c3 status, or for most types of government and grant funding, and are subject to different laws and regulations than nonprofits. For-profit status will not be addressed in this book.)

The second step is to secure federal IRS 501c3 status, which is the tax designation that makes donations to your organization deductible, and is required for foundation gifts, most grants you may apply for, and many other forms of funding the garden could receive. It is necessary to have this tax status so that donors who choose to support your organization can claim the deduction if that is their motivation for giving.

If the community garden will be part of an existing 501c3 organization, you don't need to worry about this status. If your garden is not part of another organization, is very small, or doesn't have the resources to work with professionals to file for federal status, there is the option of getting the benefits of 501c3 status without the paperwork (which can be time consuming and expensive.) This option is called fiscal sponsorship. Essentially, it allows your organization the benefits of 501c3 status via partnership with another 501c3 organization. Oftentimes a fiscal sponsor shares a similar mission to your own. There are also organizations with the express mission to provide fiscal sponsorship for new or small nonprofits unable to, or not desiring to, secure their own federal status.

A successful fiscal sponsor partnership not only gives your organization the benefits of 501c3 status, but often provides some benefit to the organization providing the sponsorship as well. Benefits could be as simple as public association with your organization to a small percentage of any funds you raise. A general percentage is 5 to 15 percent, with the reason ostensibly being that any monies raised by your group will flow through the fiscal sponsor, so they may have some administrative or accounting work to do to get the money to you. Fiscal sponsors are responsible for setting up separate checking accounts for sponsoree funds, accounting for those funds in audits, and maintaining other financial best practices. There is also a level of general oversight required—to make sure you're living up what you said you would do with grant funds received through the fiscal sponsorship. The sponsoring organization is technically on the hook should your organization not spend grant monies appropriately. This fiduciary oversight is the responsibility of the fiscal sponsor and will require administrative time on their part.

If you believe you will want to raise funds requiring 501c3 status but don't want to file independently, research and find a good fiscal sponsor ahead of time. Sometimes the relationship building takes a while: the fiscal sponsor will want to make sure your mission and their mission are in agreement; you may be required to provide paperwork or documentation; and meetings with, or approvals from, their board may be necessary. Often nonprofit boards meet on a quarterly basis, so your need for a fiscal sponsor and the sponsoring organization's schedule may not be in concert. In other words, plan ahead.

The main thing to remember is this: you're not alone. There may be a lot to learn about state nonprofit status, federal 501c3 status, boards, and the other legalities that go into running your organization, but you will find as you research the best options for your group that there are helpful local resources available. Most metropolitan areas have groups that can aid start-up nonprofits in making important decisions around the type of nonprofit status the organization should secure. Organizations and professionals will also be able to assist you with board development and other necessary business functions. Search for groups like Executive Service Corps, Donors Forum, SCORE, or Business and Professional People for the Public Interest.

Nonprofit Cows Say MOU

There's a saying, "A verbal agreement isn't worth the paper it is written on." As with any partnership, a written agreement is a good idea so that everyone can work through their expectations ahead of time, and come to an understanding on the conditions of the partnership.

An MOU (Memorandum of Understanding) is the nonprofit version of what is otherwise known in the corporate world as a contract or business agreement. While legal liability may or may not be involved, an MOU outlines what two or more organizations are agreeing to do together. MOUs are usually negotiated and approved by a governing board or leadership of the agreeing organizations. Simple or fancy, the process of working through an MOU will determine what each party is agreeing to do and the consequences for nonperformance. An MOU can outline the markers for a successful partnership, as well as define exit clauses and other actions or milestones to review the terms of the agreement or end the relationship.

ELEMENTS OF AN MOU

MOUs can be used for all types of agreements—space or land usage, partnership agreements, and fiscal sponsorships just to name a few. They are, essentially, a great way to come to agreement and document what you are agreeing to do with another organization. The steps taken to define the terms of an MOU can also give you a sneak preview of what the process of working with another organization might be like: Are they timely in replying to you? Are they willing to do everything they said in meetings, now that things are being documented? How do they react when you disagree on some terms? If they refuse to put anything in writing, that might be cause to decide not to proceed with a partnership. Much like the work your community did together to determine a mission statement, the back-and-forth with an MOU process can deepen a partnership or reveal fissures that need to be either mended or walked away from.

If your MOU will be legally binding, and not just an outlined agreement, as with any legal document, you should have an attorney or other legal professional help you draft or, at least, review it.

MOUs are unique to every situation and can be as long or as short as both parties feel comfortable with. Generally, these are the elements involved.

⇒ PARTIES

This component explains the organizations involved in the agreement, their names, addresses, legal status or corporate structure, and in which city and state the agreement is happening.

⇒ INTENT

An overview of what the MOU is for and what the parties intend to do together.

⇒ TERM

Explains the duration of the agreement.

⇒ RESPONSIBILITIES

This is the meat of the MOU, where the project is outlined and all parties define what they will do.

BOARDS AND OTHER LEADERSHIP TEAMS

If you apply for state or federal nonprofit status, you will need a board of directors. Most states require at least a three-person board—president, treasurer, and secretary—but it varies, so do some research to determine what your state requires.

As with most things related to the IRS, answers are rarely simple—and this is true for the question of how big the board should be. In this book's Resources section, you'll find IRS links that will provide information on board size and responsibilities. Keep in mind that the point of a board is fiscal and organizational oversight as well as governance, and every organization's board setup and requirements are tailored to the organization itself. Boards often start out small and grow over time as the needs of the organization evolve. Regardless of

FINANCIAL RESPONSIBILITIES

While financial responsibilities could be outlined merely in the responsibilities area, to keep things simple, they are often called out as a separate section. If there are no financial responsibilities—be sure to spell that out as well! There should be no ambiguity in the MOU. If you are drafting an MOU for fiscal sponsorship, this is the area where fiscal elements are clearly defined.

LIABILITY AND RISK SHARING

This area outlines any insurance or other liability issues, as well as who is managing them as they relate to the agreement and mishaps that may occur. An organization should never claim liability over something that it has no control over. Before you go too far with the MOU process, it is good to make sure your would-be partner has insurance or other liability coverage that they agree to provide. This includes your organization as well.

DISCLAIMERS

This is an area where you can outline what you and your partner are *not* doing. For example, you may be agreeing to use space, but the other organization is disclaiming that they will not make any improvements on the space.

CONFLICT RESOLUTION

This section outlines the steps to be taken if something goes wrong and parties need to resolve a dispute. Conflicts and the need to resolve them could develop around many things related to a partnership. Agreeing to have regular meetings to discuss the health and progress of the project, and formalizing how to decide when to go to mediation, or seek legal recourse on conflicts, are examples of possible scenarios.

MISCELLANEOUS

This final section often includes provisos for legalese such as how the agreement is binding, how it presides over previous agreements, and other related legal language.

SIGNATURES

Partnering organizations may have bylaws indicating how many board members need to sign such an agreement. Generally an executive director or another leader from each organization may sign an MOU. Depending on your organization, your board may need to formally approve MOUs before they are signed.

the size or how long the board has been established, members should be involved and interested in the activities of the organization to the extent of their ability. At the very least, they should have oversight and buy-in on large decisions and financial matters. Board members also have a personal legal liability to vouch for the fiscal management of the organization.

If you are a small garden organization, a board of three to five people should offer enough governance to oversee and support your mission. The board members may or may not be involved in the day-to-day operation of the garden, or even decide to garden; they may be more of an oversight body to provide outside perspective on a separate leadership team's decisions for the organization.

Board members—generally a president, vice president, and treasurer—serve as officers of the corporation, although anyone on the board could be designated an officer. Each officer is required to sign legal documents, such as contracts, MOUs, or other legally binding agreements, and provide a level of responsibility for the organization's actions if an issue were to be brought to court. If you have board members that come from a corporation and are serving on your board as part of their professional development, their employers may require the garden organization to have directors and operators insurance. This insurance protects board members—and by extension their employers—from any legal or financial repercussions during their board tenure.

Aside from governance, one of the main roles of many boards is fundraising. This could include seeking out funders, introducing them to the organization, exploring possible donations from personal or family resources, and participating in fundraising efforts. Many organizations make some fiscal commitment a requirement of board membership—requiring potential board members to pony up a set dollar amount before being allowed on the board, or guaranteeing introductions to prospective donors or others groups that will potentially fulfill a certain quota.

If your organization doesn't have nonprofit status, it is still a wise idea to have a board or leadership team involved in your group's activities because, much like the garden itself, a community of doers has a lot more to offer than a single, lone leader. Plus, it is more fun to have comrades who share an interest in the garden's success.

LIVING BY THE (BY)LAWS

Any nonprofit status requiring a board will also require bylaws to govern that board and, by extension, the organization in general. Bylaws are a series of, well, laws. They govern how the organization will behave and what actions to take should agreed–upon behavior not happen. Bylaws can be simple or complex, and really reflect the nature of your organization. They are required to be part of your application for state and federal nonprofit status.

For the purposes of application and compliance with nonprofit status, bylaws can include the number and titles of board members, frequency of elections, terms for removing people from the board, and terms of fiscal oversight. If the organization is small, or doesn't need state or federal nonprofit status, bylaws are still a good idea. As with most things regarding your group, they should be decided upon communally.

FINANCING YOUR PROJECT: PUTTING THE FUN IN FUNDRAISING

Chances are, the largest expenses you will encounter with the garden will come during the initial building phase. All that soil, lumber, and infrastructure cost money! But whatever you're spending organization funds on, you'll need to be prepared to tell the story of your garden—and what you're doing with your budget—to potential donors, sponsors, and funders. Here is where the community work on the mission questionnaire and mission statement developed in your initial meetings takes on another important role. Share this foundational information and use it as a guiding principle, as you create the communication vehicles necessary to convince people or organizations to fund your garden program.

Funding is available from many sources. That being said, finding those resources and understanding if they're a good fit for your organization can be another thing. Local and state governments, foundations, corporations, and service organizations are some of the many groups set up to distribute funds to organizations. They are often not publicized, so you need to know where to look. This is where a volunteer with expertise in fundraising can really come in handy. These people are called development directors or simply fundraisers. Don't be shy—ask the members of your garden community if they or someone they know can offer these skills to help out.

Chances are your funding won't come from a single source. You need to look at your budget needs and identify a variety of potential revenue sources to pay for the program. Knowing your budget needs and the types of funding you can target will comprise what is called a development plan; and it is a good idea to talk about fundraising and your development plan frequently throughout the year (at least quarterly), so you can stay current on applications and research for these funds. Creating a list of fundraising sources and channels early in the year will help your community work collectively toward meeting the fiscal goals for running and maintaining the garden.

Often, the types of funds you can apply for will be influenced by your nonprofit status or if you have a fiscal sponsor. Assuming you are a relatively small, new program without 501c3 status or a fiscal sponsor, here are some basic types of funding around which you can build your development plan.

Events and Social Media

Fundraising events come in all shapes and sizes. The easiest type is a sale. Plant sales, seed sales, bake sales, garage sales—all are excellent for stocking your coffers. Keep in mind that people like to buy something at a fundraiser. Even if your bake-sale cookies aren't worth their ten-dollar price tag, it allows the buyer to feel good about supporting your organization while getting something fun in return. Any concept that gets people interested in helping is a good thing; they may spread the word about the fundraiser to their friends and families. Fundraising itself is a community-building activity, so involve as many people as possible in the process. Be sure to research any requirements your organization might have to pay sales tax on items you sell.

Fundraising has taken a quantum leap in recent years due to social media sites and online platforms for crowd-sourced funding, such as Kickstarter or Ioby. Using one of these Internet-based tools will help you tell the story of your garden, and can potentially reach a much larger audience—the "crowd" in crowd-sourced funding—beyond your local community. And with the simplicity of sharing information through social media, your members can easily be engaged to help spread the word about the garden's fundraising efforts, too.

Member funding

The people involved in the garden are naturally the ones most likely to be interested in its long-term success. Many gardens finance all or part of their operation through membership fees. If you go that route, keep fees in line with the economics of your neighborhood and gardening community. In low-income neighborhoods, a $75 fee might be a barrier to entry for people wanting to participate, whereas the same fee might not be an issue in a high-end area. As with most garden questions, the best way to find out what your community can manage is to ask them. Some gardens have a suggested donation model for membership fees, often in a range between $15 and $100 per year. Share the garden budget with your group and together, figure out a fee structure that works for everyone. In programs where gardener contributions are the main funding source, there is often a tricky balance between the money you need to build the garden and what your members can afford. Also remember that as stated earlier, you might not be able to do everything you want the first year. Don't break the budget or your garden will suffer. Phasing has its advantages and patience is a necessity not only in gardening but also in building a successful, long-running community garden.

You can also offer a scholarship model, in which more affluent participants can help cover the costs of gardeners who may not be able to afford membership fees. You may be surprised by how supportive your community of gardeners will be once they know what's needed. Never be afraid to ask for their input and support.

Cash and In-Kind Donations

Get used to asking individuals, organizations, and local businesses for cash donations. Most people expect this type of request from non-profits, no matter how uncomfortable it may seem to you. If you don't have 501c3 status or a fiscal sponsor, you must make it clear that donations are not tax deductible, but don't worry—a tax deduction is often not the biggest motivation for a donation. Moral of the story: don't be afraid to ask, no matter what your nonprofit status, and be prepared to be delighted by the response.

Not all support comes in the form of cash. Many companies are very willing to donate materials or services to your program in lieu of dollars. Useful donations might come in the form of garden equipment, soil, tools, or other necessities. Don't overlook asking for services such as a front-end loader and operator to spread woodchips, or a CPA to help with your year-end taxes. When approaching an organization or business about in-kind donations, have a wish list of items you need ahead of time. By providing this list to potential in-kind donors, they can easily see how best they can participate in your garden.

Sponsorships

Hand-in-hand with in-kind donations and receiving support from businesses is the concept of sponsorship. Companies may be willing to give you resources in exchange for expanding their customer base by association with your garden. This goodwill, or halo effect, can translate into dollars for your sponsor in the long run, making their connection with your garden profitable as well as altruistic.

Sponsorships often involve posting the company's name, logo, and web address where gardeners or other community members will see it; in effect, associating the company with your good cause. This is often in the form of signage, logos on T-shirts, and company recognition on a website or printed materials.

And a word of caution about sponsorships: make sure the company has the same values you espouse in your community. If your organization teaches people to grow their own food organically, a chemical fertilizer company might be a conflict of interest or at least undermine your mission. If your program helps people in food deserts to grow their own food, a high-end consumer brand might not be a good fit. You'll need to look at each potential sponsor on a case-by-case basis to make sure the partnership is advantageous to both parties and reflects and supports the values of each organization. When in doubt, always refer to your mission statement.

As with donors, sponsors sometimes like to buy something or be associated with a specific element of your program. If you have a membership-driven organization, perhaps a sponsor can fund some scholarships. Or if you have a food pantry program, a sponsor might add to your produce donation with a matching food donation. Get creative with sponsors so the relationship is mutually beneficial. You get the resources you need to make your garden happen, and your sponsor gets the goodwill of helping out your cause in a creative, newsworthy way— a win-win.

PROTECTING YOUR ORGANIZATION

Gardening is not the most dangerous of activities, it's true. But things can happen in your garden that might injure people or their property. Hopefully, nothing is so serious that a "sorry that happened" and a hug won't remedy the situation, but you never know. We live in a litigious world, so some coverage to protect your organization is a prudent thing. Don't panic, though. This all may sound like heavy-duty stuff to deal with. Don't let it freak you out—just do it.

To protect your garden from liability, you will want to speak with an attorney—hopefully someone on your board or a pro bono resource—to review your liability policies and any materials you create for participating gardeners to sign. An attorney can also help you draft these policies if you are starting from scratch. By having your liability bases covered, you not only protect your organization but you educate your gardeners and their associates on the rules of the garden as well as your seriousness about the health and longevity of the program. People will appreciate this foresight. It is better to be up front and proactive about potential issues than to have to backpedal if something serious happens.

Liability Insurance

Put liability insurance into your program budget. Like most insurances, you don't need it until you need it—but then, you *really* need it. Oftentimes, new or small organizations have a difficult time getting or affording liability insurance for their garden space. Insurance you don't have to pay for is often one of the benefits of participating in a large, citywide community garden program, as they usually have a blanket policy that covers each participating garden. If you have to contribute at all, the premiums are smaller per garden due to the number of participants. You can also check with your local carrier (start with someone you personally have a policy with) to find liability insurance. If you're a solo garden, joining the American Community Gardening Association (ACGA) will be beneficial. It provides affordable access to liability insurance for member organizations. Recommended garden coverage is $1 million per incident.

GRANTS AND GRANT-WRITING TIPS

Many small grants are available to community gardens, and often, they have simple online forms. Here are some steps to help with your grant-writing success.

Do research. Use simple Google search terms such as "grants community gardens Philadelphia." Once you find funding in your area, read the guidelines carefully. Don't waste time applying for a grant if it isn't appropriate. If the funder supports school gardens, you may reason that because you are a community garden and it is kind of the same thing because you have some kids in your garden, don't apply. It's unlikely that they will fund you. You have to clearly fit the grant guidelines.

Meet the application deadline. The deadline is the deadline, and your application will not be considered if it is submitted late.

Don't provide documents or information they didn't ask for. Do give them the documents and information they require, or have a really good reason why it's missing.

Read all the way through the questions before filling in answers. Sometimes the questions can seem redundant. Answer the question that is asked.

For grants that don't include questions to answer, provide a short document. The required length will usually be in the guidelines. If there is no maximum length, shorter is better. Shoot for three to five pages, arranged with the following headings.

Typical Components of a Grant Proposal

⇒ **The Request**
For example: "ABC Community Garden is seeking a grant of $1,000 to expand its gardening program for local senior citizens."

⇒ **Mission and Organizational Description**
State your mission statement and add one or two additional descriptive sentences expanding on your mission.

⇒ **Purpose or Goals**
Describe what you plan on accomplishing.

⇒ **Programs**
Describe what you are actually doing with your programs.

⇒ **Activities**
Describe how you are accomplishing program goals.

⇒ **Outcomes or Objectives**
Describe the quantitative outcomes you are seeking, and provide the numbers against which you will measure the program's success.

⇒ **Evaluation**
Describe how you will determine your success in fulfilling the requirements of the grant.

⇒ **Sustainability**
Describe how the program will be funded going forward, especially if your organization doesn't get this particular grant. (Never ask a single funder to support an entire program.)

⇒ **Conclusion**
This is your opportunity to sell. Use your most heartstring-pulling language. Include photos if possible. Close with the words, "thank you."

An important thing to keep in mind: if you are borrowing land for the short term from an individual, institution, or a government organization, you generally cannot get permission or a lease without first having liability insurance. Do your homework and become a member of ACGA, or find a carrier you can afford and have that information available when you're ready to talk land.

A Safe Garden Is Everyone's Business

Your garden leadership team needs to be responsible, identifying and rectifying safety issues in the garden, particularly situations that gardeners have brought to your attention. It is imperative to fix problems as they arise—before they become issues that could harm someone. No number of signatures on documents will help in the case of negligence. If you're lucky, gardeners will take matters into their own hands and deal with worrisome or threatening situations as they come up. Setting up a formal channel for reporting garden concerns is an important step in managing and maintaining a safe and well-run garden. It is always best to empower your gardeners to feel responsible for the safety of everyone. Then it's not just you or your small group of leaders who seem to be responsible but all of the participants. It is truly a community space when the people who use the garden understand and are active in its success organizationally. This includes safety, too.

Signatures and Signage

Hold harmless waiver Many organizations create a hold harmless waiver that is mandatory for all participants to sign. During your garden registration process, you might want to have participants sign an agreement stating that they understand there may be dangers involved in participating in the garden, and that they waive any claims of legal action against the garden organization due to injury or other damages to physical property. Make it clear that signing a hold harmless waiver will apply to the member, their family, and anyone they invite onto the garden property.

Media permissions form You are going to want to document the life of your garden either for your own memories, for the garden community, or to share with potential funders. A media permissions form allows you to use anyone's image in materials related to the garden. This is another element that many gardens build into the registration process as a caveat for participation. As with the hold harmless waiver, a signed media permissions form will apply to the member, their family, and anyone they invite onto the garden property. And, of course, if you're in the garden taking pictures and members ask not to be photographed, even though they have signed a permission form, be kind and respect their wishes.

"Enter at your own risk" signage You're probably going to have some identifying signage at your garden, such as "Welcome to the XYZ Community Garden!" This is a good place to also post a notice to those who enter and have not signed a hold harmless form. Your gardeners have signed a waiver, covering themselves and anyone they've invited into the garden, but it also useful to have signage as a reminder for those covered by the hold harmless waiver as well as for passersby who might wander in to admire the amazing garden. "Enter at your own risk" signage, prominently displayed by all entrances, provides another way to cover your organization in case of an accident. If the community garden is located in a neighborhood with residents who speak a language other than English, and you have the resources, state your disclaimer in all languages that are applicable.

MANAGING THE MONEY

There will be funds associated with your garden or organization. If participants have provided support in the way of donations or membership fees, they may have an interest in understanding where the money is going and how it is supporting the organization.

Money Management Basics

The budget Some people are good at budgets and money, and some are not. If you or members of your leadership team are not money people, find a volunteer or pro bono resource that can help. A CPA or someone who does accounting as a day job will be a godsend in this process. At the very least, perhaps they can set up your accounts and budget. Then other team members can manage things moving forward. The pros can also suggest and set up reports that help you keep the community informed of the dollars involved in the program and how the money is being used.

An operating budget is your best friend. If you've worked with budgets before, you know they're more of an art than a science. Most budgets need some flexibility to manage unexpected costs, windfall donations, or other funding wins and losses. It doesn't matter whether your program is tiny or huge, a budget is a necessity. This is not only a good management practice for your leadership team; it also provides documentation that helps the community understand the health of the organization. Nobody may ask to see it, but if they do, be prepared to share. And a well-articulated budget is a requirement for most funders.

Checking account If your garden is teeny tiny, one of your leadership members can potentially manage the dollars through their personal account—providing you have a lot of oversight and a written agreement that this is all right with the organization, including what checks and balances will be required and when to determine that all dollars are accounted for. This isn't an ideal situation, but for really small, intimate gardens, it might be the easiest and least costly option.

A more practical approach is to open a checking account specific to the organization. To open a business account, you'll need your state nonprofit status or some other form of incorporation. Speak with someone at your bank of choice to determine what is required. Keep in mind when choosing banks that sometimes local banks are more likely to help with a small business account than a national banking chain might be. Small local banks are also a potential funding source; they are as invested in the community as you are. Often, having an account with a neighborhood bank is required to be eligible for any community donation funds they may have available. Larger national chains, on the other hand, might have better online support (potentially allowing multiple people to view account activity and make transactions) and generally have better reporting features. They may also offer credit cards with points systems that you can then use for purchasing supplies or other needed materials.

Collecting funds via PayPal, Square, or other payment management systems If you are working with a membership-fee structure, chances are you're going to have to have multiple ways to accept fees. Cash or checks from members work fine. But some gardeners may want to pay using a credit card, or you may be in a situation where it is difficult to meet people to get their cash or check payments. Pay-Pal is one trusted way to accept credit card funds online. It charges a service fee for managing the transaction, so keep that in mind when you're setting up your membership fees; if you're on a tight budget, and you really need every dollar your members contribute, you might have to add a small percentage to the membership fee to cover the service charge. The same is true with credit card readers like Square or Intuit GoPayment, which work on a mobile phone. They're easy to set up and very handy, but there's a fee involved with each transaction that you'll need to take into account. The garden organization will need a bank account before these services can be used, because funds collected are transferred from the service to a bank account, minus any fees.

PART THREE

MANAGING THE COMMUNITY AND THE GARDEN

5. MOBILIZING

Developing a Team of Gardeners and Volunteers

By now, you've likely gotten the message that without a community, you've just got a big garden that, doubtless, you can't maintain on your own. Volunteers, no matter where they come from, are essential to a thriving community garden. These helping hands may be those of the gardeners themselves, service organizations, corporations, or just neighbors who aren't into growing food so much but love their community and want to see it improved. Many high school programs nationwide require students to participate in a set number of service-learning hours to graduate. Churches, local businesses, and other organizations are a great source of volunteers; you shouldn't have to do much arm-twisting to get them engaged in the garden.

The trick to engaging volunteers is to include the following key elements in your management program: safety, good communication, organization, meaningful work, and, most importantly, appreciation and celebration. You may worry that rallying volunteers will be difficult, but who knows? There may be a surprising overabundance of help and interest in your garden. Everyone who contributes is part of the community and should be recognized as vital to its success.

GETTING GARDENERS SETTLED: REGISTRATION AND ORIENTATION

After all the work of organizing the community around a mission, designing and planning your space, getting all the ongoing gardening logistics worked out, and setting up a sound business structure, it is time to set your garden in motion in a major way. This is where registration and orientation come in.

Let us be grateful to people who make us happy, they are the charming gardeners who make our souls blossom.

—Proust

It's possible that you may have more potential gardeners than you have garden space. This is exciting, but if there just isn't room for everyone, you have a few options. You can create a waiting list for plots—often there is a surge of interest at the outset that wanes, opening up available garden spots. You can also suggest that folks with an interest in gardening become active volunteers. Finally, you can ask around and see if any of the registered gardeners are willing to share their space.

Registration is the process wherein people interested in becoming members of your community garden provide information and payment (if applicable). Orientation is sharing the ground rules of the physical garden with participants, so you're all on the same page.

There may be people who volunteer in the garden but don't want to actually garden. They don't necessarily have to go through this process— it is up to you to decide how to track non-gardening volunteers. But for anyone who will be gardening, information and any required fees will need to be captured. And everyone needs to understand and appreciate the rules of the garden.

Registration

Depending on the size of your garden and your payment structure, registration can be simple or complex. Some organizations simply have a paper form that people fill out and return with a check. Some organizations use an online event registration system such as Event-Brite or BrownPaperTickets to manage registration and capture all the information easily in a digital format. A benefit of online systems is that they are able to accept credit card payments without your organization having to go through the hassle of setting up special merchant accounts to do so yourself. However, online systems take a percentage of each transaction and sometimes a per transaction fee, too. Fees vary by service.

Information to Capture During Registration

⇒ First name

⇒ Last name

⇒ Address

⇒ E-mail address

⇒ Phone number(s)

⇒ Names and ages of participating gardeners

⇒ Best way to contact gardeners

⇒ Level of garden knowledge

⇒ Special skills gardeners can contribute

⇒ Affiliations gardeners may have with local partners or your organization

⇒ Any other information you find valuable for the administration of the garden and your garden organization

Registration is also a great time to have gardeners sign hold harmless and media permissions agreements. With online systems, the hold harmless and media permissions can be built into the process, so registrants must agree to them before the registration process can be completed. It works much like online terms and conditions, in which you have to agree before you can proceed with an online purchase or, for example, Wi-Fi use).

Orientation

Orientation can be as simple as handing out and discussing a list of rules at registration, or as formal as a special meeting. Many organizations require live orientations to make sure that everyone receives the same information regarding the garden. However it's accomplished, and however difficult it may be to get everyone together, making sure every gardening member knows and understands your agreed-upon protocols is one of the most important ways you can help ensure the long-term success of your garden.

Set a Positive Tone

Orientation information should mirror the garden rules you want your members to live by. Think this through very carefully. You want to present enough meaningful material that people can fully participate, but not have the orientation so rule-heavy that participants roll their eyes and ignore what you are saying. Tone is also very important. Make your language positive and friendly. People tend to ignore presentations with lots of "don'ts". This is an excellent time to establish an upbeat, involved foundation for the garden.

SAFETY FIRST!

Before getting into the fun of working with your ambitious community to build the garden, and before anyone begins gardening on the property, be sure to read and address the business of setting up and running a community organization discussed in chapter 4, where the need for liability insurance and hold harmless waivers are explained.

The liability insurance covers accidents that may happen on site, and the waiver indemnifies, or protects, your organization from litigation should an injury occur. While most volunteers are good-natured and not looking for a lawsuit, it is a best practice to make sure everyone signs a waiver.

Waivers can be signed in advance, when registering for membership or registering as a volunteer. If you use an online tool, such as EventBrite or BrownPaperTickets, for people to sign up for volunteer

INFORMATION TO CONSIDER SHARING AT ORIENTATION

➡ **ABOUT YOUR ORGANIZATION**

Include your mission, a bit about the garden's history and any partners you are working with.

➡ **VISITOR OR GUEST POLICIES**

Discuss your policies for visitors in the garden; encourage members to greet visitors and let them know whether visitors are welcome, or unwelcome, to harvest vegetables.

➡ **GARDENING APPROACHES**

Mention your policy about organic gardening (if you have one) and discuss any special gardening philosophies (such as permaculture) which participants are required to employ.

➡ **PROGRAMS**

Discuss special programs or partners, how such programs work, and how the gardeners are expected or not expected to participate. For example, if a portion of your garden is donated to a local food and nutrition partner, explain how that system works.

➡ **VOLUNTEERING**

Discuss your volunteer needs. If you have a mandatory hours program (see p. 115), discuss that and how gardeners are expected to fulfill these hours.

➡ **ACCESS**

Discuss any issues related to getting into the garden, such as how to use the lock, making sure the gates are locked when the last person leaves, and closing gates when people are alone in the garden for security reasons. If your garden doesn't have a fence, talk about your policies for managing theft (if you care), and policies around harvest of vegetables.

➡ **COMMUNITY AREAS**

Talk about group responsibilities for common areas, such as picking up trash and pulling weeds. If you have a trash receptacle, discuss this. If you ask your gardeners to take their trash home with them, discuss this. Encourage gardeners to police the perimeter of the garden for trash or weeds.

➡ **SPECIAL EVENTS**

If you will be having special events (or want to have special events), talk about other ways the garden can be used and encourage gardeners to help come up with or manage events.

➡ **CONSEQUENCES OF NON-PARTICIPATION**

You will have instances of people not doing what they agreed to do. Expect it. Decide prior to registration what the consequences will be for such issues as unweeded plots, unharvested food, and members who don't fulfill mandatory volunteer hours. Will they be kicked out of the garden or not allowed to return the following season? Will their plot be tended or harvested after a notification and a waiting period? Will the plot be assigned to someone on a waiting list? Let gardeners know ahead of time what to expect, so there are no misunderstandings. And don't set up a system you won't be able to enforce because it will ruin your credibility moving forward. Also remember that this is a community garden—it's not the end of the world if someone leaves, as people do in any community. Don't make a bigger deal of it than need be; life happens and everyone needs a little forgiveness once in a while. Set a matter-of-fact tone for these situations up front.

⇨ TOOLS

If you have shared tools, talk about usage and return policies. If you have a shed or storage area, discuss access and how it is secured.

⇨ WATER

Cover your watering setup. Encourage people to keep water areas tidy and to conserve water by shutting off hoses, if applicable. Talk about water etiquette—don't take down someone's prize tomato as you're pulling the hose to your plot. If you have an irrigation system, discuss this.

⇨ OTHER FEATURES

Include anything else gardeners need to know. If you have a compost program, explain how that works. If you have chickens in your garden, explain the rules for interacting with them or gathering eggs. If you have berries or fruit trees that are a shared asset, discuss what gardeners are allowed to harvest. Your garden will be unique—this is the time to make sure all elements of the collective dream are nurtured and appreciated by the community.

⇨ DOGS

Determine if you will allow dogs in the garden. Many gardens do not for sanitary reasons. This makes dog owners very sad, because they think their dog is special and would never pee on anyone's vegetables. A good compromise is to find a spot in the common area, away from where food is growing, that dogs can be tied up or hang out with their owners.

⇨ HOW TO REPORT ISSUES

Remind members that they have signed a hold harmless waiver, and that it is everyone's responsibility to keep the gardens safe. Let gardeners know how to report issues or concerns. If you are in a neighborhood with crime issues, you may want to talk to your local police before orientation about providing additional safety instructions. Law enforcement agencies are almost always willing to help, and starting a relationship with the local authorities can go a long way toward a positive community experience.

⇨ KEEPING IN TOUCH

Remind gardeners how to communicate in general. Encourage gardeners to send questions through e-mail, to post on your social media venues, or to call someone. If the garden is part of an organization that has a physical office (like a community center or a senior facility), let gardeners know when they are welcome to come by and to whom they should talk.

⇨ SAY THE MAGIC WORDS: THANK YOU

Remember, your gardeners may also be your main volunteer base. They don't have to be there. They are choosing to be part of the community and need to feel welcome and appreciated. Encourage them to chime in with any additional rules or guidelines they think might be useful over the course of the season. And, as the garden community matures, be open to revisit and adjust the rules accordingly.

⇨ REINFORCE ORIENTATION WITH SIGNAGE

You can turn your orientation document into a sign. Post it in a very visible place—or several visible places—to remind gardeners and reinforce the rules of engagement.

events, the hold harmless waiver can be part of that process. Much like software licensing, users can't complete the sign-up process without agreeing to the waiver. If you have a manual registration or volunteer sign-up process, you will have to provide printed waivers and keep track of them in a safe place. You will also want a list available on site of those who have signed waivers for volunteer activities. Sometimes people who haven't signed up online or in advance will show up on volunteer days. In these cases, it is good to have paper copies of the waiver on site for people to sign.

When young people under eighteen years of age want to volunteer or garden without their families, waivers need to be signed by a parent or guardian. If you are working with a school group or another youth-oriented program for a volunteer day, ask the person in charge if they have an existing waiver in place and if it will cover volunteers on the community garden property. Request a copy of the paperwork for good measure and keep it on file for your records. It is also a good idea to have an adult related to the volunteering organization on site to provide students with supervision and direction. Often paperwork is required as proof of service-learning hours, so, in addition to supervision, having a helper from the providing organization present during the work is a good practice. It will be helpful to you at the end of a busy day when you want to wrap things up and lots of papers need to be signed. The supervisor can do this, freeing you for other tasks.

A safe worksite is essential at all times—and clearly necessary during the building of the garden's physical structures. Volunteers helping to construct, for example, raised beds, will most likely be engaged with power tools, sharp instruments, electricity, and other materials that my cause hazards. Make sure all volunteers have the proper skills to handle the tools they're working with, and that proper safety gear is used. If you're borrowing power from a neighbor, or using a generator to power drills, make sure extension cords do not get wet or sit in water. Even the simple task of raking wood chips can have hazardous consequences, so instruct volunteers to not leave tools on the ground. We've all seen that old cartoon: someone steps on a rake, the handle whizzes up into the person's face, and clobber stars burst out, spinning around the victim's head. This is only funny in cartoons and can cause serious injury. If this happens to you—as it has to me one too many times—there will be nothing funny about the pain you experience.

Drinking water is crucial! Especially on hot days. Have plenty of water available for your volunteers. It is extra nice to provide lunch, but that's optional, depending on the length of the workday. During sign-up, you can ask people to bring their own beverages but, inevitably, not everyone will remember, so be prepared. Don't be discouraged about these issues, just think ahead.

STRIKE WHILE THE IRON IS HOT: GENERATING AND MAINTAINING INTEREST

This may be stating the obvious, but the height of enthusiasm and volunteerism for your garden will be as you're building it, or in the spring, or both.

For example, my garden hometown, Chicago, is in USDA zone 6a. Our growing season is relatively short (and hot), while the winters are long, bone-chillingly cold, and trying. By the time spring comes around, people are manic to get outside and move. Because our program builds large gardens each spring, when it comes to recruiting volunteers, the Chicago winter is one of our greatest allies! If you live in another part of the country, the best time for garden planting and building might not be so easily defined; winter weather may, or may not, be a significant ally in motivating your volunteers. Fall is also a great time to build a garden. With a lot of harvest and cleanup chores to do, and, at least in Chicago, bad weather pending, people are often excited to help wrap up the garden season for the year and get their last burst of outdoor activity.

Meaningful work is essential for a good volunteer program. From my experience, meaningful work usually involves short-term or one-time projects such as building, planting, or harvesting. Routine maintenance projects, weeding in particular, aren't as popular but are essential. Once the frenzy of building and planting is over, gardeners settle into the routines of garden maintenance, watering, and weeding their plots. If your garden is a shared garden, rather than an allotment where individuals maintain their own little slice of paradise, you'll need to set up collective watering and weeding schedules to make sure your garden thrives.

Keeping volunteers and gardeners excited about routine maintenance can be managed with a few simple tactics early in the season.

There will be times of the year, depending on your weather and seasons, when people are just tired. As much as they may love their gardens, life gets busy with holidays, vacations, kids going back to school. Sometimes just as the plants are making their final push to produce food, there is a natural wind-down of enthusiasm for the garden. This doesn't mean people have lost interest; it just means they need a little break. Luckily for all of us, hope springs eternal, a new garden season will come again, and that enthusiasm will be back in full force.

ON-SITE VOLUNTEER TOOLKIT

Here's a handy list of basic materials to have during a volunteer workday.

➡ Clipboard, notepad, and pens

➡ Sign-in sheet: you want to keep track of your volunteers so you can thank them later or add them to a newsletter or other form of communication

➡ List of expected participants who have signed hold harmless waivers

➡ Hold harmless waivers for drop-ins

➡ Water: either in plastic bottles or a big container (don't forget the cups)

➡ Work gloves: get a range of sizes (bulk packages are sold at hardware and building stores)

➡ Safety goggles (for build days, when power tools are involved)

➡ Sunscreen

➡ Insect repellant

➡ Materials about your program: if passersby see a lot of action happening, they'll stop by and ask what's up. Be sure to have materials to share about your garden program so you don't have to repeat yourself numerous times and can focus on managing the volunteer project.

MAKING WORKDAYS ANYTHING BUT ROUTINE

1. **Set up regularly scheduled workdays** throughout the season and communicate them early and often. Post them in the garden, talk about them in your newsletter, send e-mails about them. However you communicate with your gardeners, train them to understand that regularly scheduled workdays are a time when the community is together, tending the garden. Also emphasize that these general maintenance tasks (such as weeding and trash pickup) are part of their duty to help keep the garden looking its best.

2. **Make workdays fun and social.** This can be a good way to get local businesses or stores involved. Ask neighboring businesses or partners to sponsor a workday with either supplies (if the partner is a hardware store, for example) or treats (if the partner is a restaurant or ice cream parlor). You can even ask local businesses to provide a coupon or free samples to hand out as a thank-you. It doesn't really matter what you do; the effort is what matters to people.

3. **Document the workdays** with photos and comments that you share through your communication channels. Make sure the photos include before and after shots, along with hardworking, smiling people.

4. **Say thank you.** This is the most important part of this entire chapter (maybe the entire book, and maybe life in general). Shake peoples' hands or hug them as they leave. Tell them their efforts have made a difference. Smile. Share the day's triumphs: "Can you believe we picked up all that trash? We couldn't have done it without you." Make a point to remember the names of all participants. Take note of the regular volunteers and send them a thank-you note or a packet of seeds—something to show that you recognize their dedication. And a little public recognition doesn't hurt, either.

But it can be a bummer when there is a big project scheduled midsummer and the heat, holidays, or vacations reduce the number of volunteers able or willing to help. Keep this in mind when you're planning a big undertaking. Strike while the gardeners are at their most eager. And don't be discouraged if you notice slumps in interest throughout the year. To everything—food harvests, enthusiasm—there is a season.

GARDEN HELPERS: MANY HANDS MAKE LIGHT WORK

I hope I didn't give the impression that the only volunteers needed are those who tend the physical garden. If you don't want to drive yourself and your leadership team crazy, all sorts of people need to be willing to step up and do lots of tasks inside and outside the garden. The more you encourage participation, the more you spread out the work, and the stronger the community becomes.

You'll need lots of behind-the-scenes team members to make your project run smoothly (or happen at all). While knowing how to use power tools, owning a truck, or teaching a workshop are vital to the life of your physical garden, people with business skills are essential to the longevity of your garden organization.

ORGANIZE A SKILLED VOLUNTEER BASE

⟹ **PROJECT OR EVENT MANAGERS**

These people can help with special activities, managing or planning workdays in the garden, or maintaining relationships or programs with partners or funders.

⟹ **DEVELOPMENT AND FUNDRAISING PROFESSIONALS**

Volunteers who work in fundraising or development will be a great asset to your team. Not only will they be aware of funding sources you may be able to tap, they also understand how to talk to funders. Also, volunteers involved with other nonprofit organizations can help you navigate the legal and governmental paperwork that may be required to evolve your organization.

⟹ **LEGAL PROFESSIONALS**

Attorneys or others in the legal field are invaluable, especially when it comes to negotiating property leases, reviewing documents, and drafting important materials like hold harmless waivers or MOUs. And, if something bad happens in your garden (heaven forbid), an attorney can provide great support and peace of mind, and perhaps mediate in a sticky situation.

⟹ **ACCOUNTANTS**

Your garden may be small, but people always get weird when money is involved. Someone with accounting skills can set up your books, even if they're basic, and help track income and expenditures so everything is on the up-and-up.

⟹ **GRAPHIC DESIGNERS**

Savvy hobby and professional designers are great for helping with web-based needs, garden signage, flyers, logos, or other ways to communicate the garden's message to the community.

⟹ **WRITING, PUBLIC RELATIONS, AND MARKETING PROFESSIONALS**

The specialized skills that PR and marketing professionals have—and their proficiency and experience with social media and how to write copy—can be an enormous help when it comes to spreading the word about your project in the community or beyond.

WORKING WITH OUTSIDE VOLUNTEER GROUPS

Depending on the size of your town or city, a local service or community organization may want to get in on the fun at the community garden. These organizations can include local groups such as Rotary or Kiwanis, fraternal organizations like the Masons or Knights of Columbus, or other service organizations. They may also be nonprofits with a service-driven mission similar to your own. Whatever their story, they may want to garden with you or provide regular work groups to help with garden maintenance. Churches and other religious organizations often have a mandate to help their communities, and working with your garden in a one-off or long-term capacity can be a great fit for both groups. Corporations interested in the well-being of their employees and looking for outside volunteer opportunities, either for individuals or groups, are now popular. High school or college students seeking service-learning hours are also a potential for positive, free labor.

The trick with a large outside group is having enough work for them. Naturally, if you're building the garden and have hundreds of cubic yards of wood chips to spread, the larger the group the better. But, as the season progresses, finding enough for a large group to do can become a challenge. There is also the issue of timing. While it is safe to guess that many of your volunteer efforts and workdays are scheduled on weekends, corporations or groups made up largely of retirees often want to do their team-building activities on weekdays. If these regular workdays don't line up with a large group's needs, it can be a challenge to work out how you can benefit from this free labor and exposure to your garden.

If you can make the timing work, the easiest (and oldest) garden task known to humanity is weeding. Every garden needs it, and it is such a low-skill chore that anyone with some sunscreen, a good pair of gloves, and a little patience can get the job done. Collecting trash around the perimeter of your garden is another simple task that often needs to be performed on a regular basis, and gives some sense of accomplishment to your volunteer crew.

If your garden is a collective (as compared to having allotment plots), watering might be something that can keep several people busy for an hour or two depending on how many hoses or watering cans you have. Also, with a collective garden, harvesting might be an option—but first ask your gardeners. Sometimes the picking is the best part for them and, after long weeks of tending, to let someone from the outside have all the fun might not sit well.

If you have more people than tasks, suggest that the service day include a lecture by a local authority on a topic agreed upon by you

HOW TO MANAGE A LARGE OUTSIDE VOLUNTEER GROUP

Communicate the mission of your organization to your point person at the volunteering organization, outlining what the tasks will be and what's expected of participants. Creating e-mails or documents covering this information might seem like busywork, but a few simple guidelines sent ahead of time will make sure everyone's expectations align, helping ensure that the day goes smoothly.

The volunteers may be eager to get their hands dirty, but is there an opportunity to do a quick pitch to them about becoming donors? Maybe even a short presentation about your program? Try to provide some additional education or information, so the time spent on your project is worthwhile for them and you.

Before

➡ Clearly communicate event details, along with the level of work involved (easy to difficult).

➡ Suggest what they should wear, and identify any materials they need to bring (such as gloves or sunscreen).

➡ Make sure the organization has signed hold harmless waivers or equivalent, for all participants.

During

➡ Sign everyone in and ensure that they have provided a hold harmless waiver.

➡ Identify supervisors, team leaders, and go-to people.

➡ Provide a list of all activities for the day, and the number of people needed for each.

➡ Have all materials which you will be providing on hand and ready.

➡ Welcome the volunteers, thank them for their time, and provide information about your program.

➡ Indicate to everyone where the bathrooms are, and where they can get water.

➡ Document the day with photos or video.

After

➡ Check that all tasks are completed.

➡ Ask volunteers to gather any provided materials and put them in one place. If you have provided materials like safety goggles or gloves, it is important to have them returned.

➡ Express your appreciation to the group on site, then send a follow up thank-you note or call the project coordinator to again say how grateful you are for their participation.

➡ Make sure to recognize the organization with a thank-you in your communication channels.

VOLUNTEER PERSONALITIES

Once the frenzy of spring wears off and people settle into a routine, you'll start to observe some personality types of the volunteers in your garden. Just recognize that a variety of commitment levels and cyclical waves of interest are normal.

Garden Zombies I mean this in the nicest way! These folks love their garden like a zombie loves fresh brains! They spend as much time as possible tending their own plot, as well as the plots of others, and helping with garden chores; often they are the first ones active in the spring and the last in the fall helping to clean up. They are self-motivated and fix problems before they become problems, or have great suggestions. They're dependable and vital to a healthy garden, and often become garden leaders. (They may also have the tendency to get irate when others aren't as passionate about the garden as they are.)

Middle-of-the-Roaders These folks are excited at the beginning and help occasionally throughout the season. They may have demanding jobs or family situations preventing them from helping more. Time is often an issue. By listing required garden chores in an easily accessible place, these folks can contribute when they can, as they can. They are sometimes great resources for ongoing, low-skill work that they can do at their own pace and timing.

The Well-Intentioned This group thinks the garden is a great idea—in theory. But when the enthusiasm of spring is over, they're on to other things. On the bright side, their flame may burn white hot in the beginning, so you can get a lot of work out of them in the early stages.

The Obligated At times there will be groups or individuals in your garden (usually young people) who have gotten wrangled into being there for reasons beyond their control. They might be part of a youth program with a community service component, or students who have service-learning hours they need to complete—and may be less-than-enthusiastic volunteers. Perfect for these individuals are easy tasks such as watering or weeding.

Will Work for Food It is amazing what you can get out of people when food is involved. Keep this in mind during the planning of group workdays. Sometimes you can partner with a local restaurant or grocery store to be a sponsor of a workday by providing lunch, snacks, or beverages. They may also provide additional helpers through advertising your workday at their business.

and the service organization. Alternatively, you or one of the members of your leadership team can talk about the mission of your project. Or, if you have community partners, maybe they could use part of the large organization for a task. You can use the garden as a meeting spot, with smaller groups spreading out across the neighborhood, performing tasks. After the event is over, everyone can regroup at the garden to celebrate.

Before you rule out working with a large organization, especially a corporate group, keep in mind that they often have funds allocated for employee-volunteer events. If you are contacted about such an event, don't be shy to ask if they'd like to cover the expenses of a special project. This might be a great chance to get the labor and dollars for that pergola your gardeners have been dreaming about.

Mandatory Volunteer Hours. An Oxymoron?

There are programs that require gardeners to volunteer for a set number of hours per season. This is often the case with food pantry or other communal projects, where the food is either given away or shared collectively. In other instances, the hours are in lieu of program fees (in the case of those who need a scholarship). Sometimes mandatory hours are merely a strategy to ensure that work within the garden is performed throughout the season, with everyone being required to contribute a set amount of time.

The upside of this approach is that, at least in the situation where hours are in exchange for program fees, gardeners receiving the scholarship have some skin in the game and a sense of contributing to the garden in a meaningful way. The downside is the time it takes to manage such a system.

Depending on the size of the garden and the number of gardeners involved, a mandatory hours program could become a management nightmare. If you implement a program like this, the volunteers managing it need to have the stamina to carry through with it all season long. Should you implement a program only to have it fall apart mid-season, your credibility for such a program has been damaged for the following season. Develop the guidelines around the program, including the consequences of not fulfilling mandatory hours. Are the gardeners penalized or excluded from the garden the following season? Is there a financial penalty? Be careful when setting up programs like this—you (or a volunteer managing the program) don't want to be seen as "the boss." Nobody wants that.

Some mandatory hours programs are on an honor system. Gardeners are required to track their own involvement against a suggested minimum. These programs can work, in that they reinforce the community element of the garden—everyone has to take part for the garden to succeed—but an individual or team of individuals doesn't have to be the heavy and make sure everyone is doing their part.

6. THE YEAR-ROUND COMMUNITY

Keeping It Fun

There are many wonderful things about gardens. They tune us in to the seasons of the year, they help us understand patience, and as the year progresses and we experience bounty, drought, drama, and excitement, they give us joy and make us feel alive. By holding activities within the garden that support and celebrate the seasons, the volunteers, gardeners, and community members become more invested in all the lessons and joys that the community garden offers. Plan activities to engage the community inside and outside the garden, from one season to the next, throughout the year.

PROGRAMS GROW WITH THE GARDEN

With the Peterson Garden Project, we wanted to create a space where gardeners had a place to learn how to grow food alongside their neighbors. What we didn't want was to have them running in, harvesting their lettuce, and running out again. In our situation—a busy urban environment—we knew that to engage our community fully, we had to use the garden to solve other challenges in our gardeners' lives.

The easiest thing we did in the garden was to fulfill our mission: providing educational opportunities for gardeners. In our first year, this involved basic gardening instruction in the spring, to get people comfortable with growing. We figured that gardening isn't that difficult, so once people had a place to grow food, along with some basic instruction, they'd get started and we could go from there.

After our first year, we learned that getting people started in the spring was not enough. Slowly, we added additional educational sessions with instructions on harvesting, insect control, and other relevant topics. Eventually, we started sharing cooking tips because we found that although people were really into learning to grow food,

We are all dependent on one another, every soul of us on earth.

—G. B. Shaw

they often didn't know what to do with their food once it was ready to harvest.

As the needs of our community changed, and as we collectively learned the needs of the gardeners, our programming and offerings evolved to meet those needs. When you're just starting out, you can only do what you can do, and you have to begin somewhere. It is important to do your best with your new garden and also to not bite off more than you can chew. Whatever activities you pick to keep your gardeners connected, do them well. It is better to do a few things that have awesome results, than a lot of activities of minimal value that wear your volunteers out. Remember your mission and keep your projects on track. And as the garden matures and more leaders arise to take on new projects, integrate them when the time seems right. Don't rush the garden or the community.

SEASONAL FUN: ACTIVITIES AND PROGRAMS

Each season brings its challenges and opportunities. The needs of the growing season naturally dictate potential activities or programs, and during your busy building and planting season, there are lots of reasons for people to be together in the garden. But as the garden slows down, the opportunities for people to congregate and build community become less obvious, so you will want to be creative about providing rationale and opportunities to get together. Local or national holidays can provide a backbone for events or celebrations. And the needs of the garden organization itself might provide fodder for meetings or other gatherings.

Winter

Usually when you think of the start of the garden year, spring is the first season that comes to mind. However, those long days of winter (at least in the north) are when gardeners start longing for sunnier days that warm the soil, and all the fresh vegetables they will grow.

As seed catalogs start appearing in January, a funny thing happens. Even though your gardeners know they have a finite amount of space, the imaginary garden expands and expands to accommodate all the interesting seed varieties available in the catalogs. Inevitably, someone with a 4-by-8-foot plot will have enough seeds for an acre farm. Plan a seed swap to bring the gardeners together to reconnect and get their excitement going for the growing season ahead (and to deal with all that excess seed inventory).

Seed swaps provide benefits and opportunities. Your gardeners have a chance to share seeds, garden stories, and tips. To keep things economical and productive for participants of all income levels, seed swaps provide a way to stock up on seeds at little or no cost. When gardeners reconnect after busy winter holidays, there's the opportunity for more seasoned gardeners to take positions of leadership with new gardeners, offering advice or other helpful tips. It is also another opportunity to recruit volunteers and build excitement for the coming season.

Spring

Spring is a no-brainer for community involvement. Your building, planting, or education activities will be abuzz with activity; if you have done a good job recruiting and advertising your community garden, there will most likely be an abundance of help and interest. This busy season may not require any special events or other activities, since the nature of the season will bring people together in the garden.

To maximize the positive energy, however, now is a good time to implement a recognition program for volunteers. At Peterson Garden Project, we created a Volunteer of the Week program. You'll need to determine the frequency of this recognition event for your garden—you can award a volunteer-of-the-week, -month, or -season. We began by working with a local hardware store close to many of our gardens. You can work with other local businesses to find suitable prizes—free gardening tools, pizza, or ice cream, for example. Our partnership with the hardware store involved a free pair of work gloves for the honored volunteer in exchange for the store name being mentioned every time we promoted Volunteer of the Week. The hardware store also offered a 10 percent discount to all of our gardeners. Over time, we were also able to influence the garden products and brands the store offered; we talked them into carrying open-pollinated seeds because of demand from our gardeners.

Summer

Summer is when things start to slow down. The frenzy of planting is over and gardeners have settled into routine maintenance tasks. People are no longer required to be together at a specific time to accomplish a goal—the gardens are planted, beginners have been educated and assisted, and volunteers have pitched in to get the garden in prime shape. Summer is when it is wise to plan social events in the garden, to keep people engaged, and to make the garden a community hub for activities and socializing. Gardens seem to attract artists of all kinds, so think of summer as a time to let the creative energy of your community come out to play.

In each of our Peterson Garden Project spaces, we build a stage. In its simplest form, the stage is a gathering place for kids in the garden to create their own nightly dramas and comedies, often performing for themselves and anyone who cares to watch. One garden space shows movies on a wall, using electricity from the next-door auto center. Visitors have told us the garden has changed the area from a dangerous place to people walking around, enjoying events, and gardening night and day.

We also invite acoustic musicians to perform in the garden, which led to a brilliant idea! If people are coming to the garden for music, why not have local Master Gardeners on hand to answer questions? This gave birth to our award-winning Music and Master Gardener series that we have offered every year since the project began. Fourth of July is the unofficial end to the frenzy of spring planting. We find this to be a great time to start the Music and Master Gardener series. One night of music a month is enough to bring people together to enjoy each other's company and enjoy all the garden has to offer on a beautiful summer night.

Fall

The gardens are winding down, at least in the north, and the gardeners in your community might start to feel melancholy because the season is over. It is always nice to have a big event in the fall to celebrate your collective accomplishment. It can be a time to recognize super volunteers or potential leaders for next year. It can also be an opportunity to reinforce your end-of-season, or winter, gardening rules. If you have a garden cleanup scheduled for the near future, make a volunteer recruitment announcement. Or, better still, if you decide to get together for a meal, talk to people while their mouths are full so they can't say no!

SPRING: VOLUNTEER GET TOGETHER

People *love* to be acknowledged! A program like this builds a culture of appreciation in your garden and sets the tone for a positive community focus. It's also an added opportunity to expand your community; to communicate with the public, local businesses, and other organizations.

Before

⮕ Determine what the desired outcome of your volunteer event should be. Is it merely social or to thank people? Will you be outlining project goals for the next season, or soliciting ideas or assistance?

⮕ Be prepared to answer questions beyond those related to your volunteers. Depending on how widely you advertise your volunteer event, you might have people showing up who have neither volunteered nor gardened with you. This is an opportunity to provide information about your program. You might also find that potential community partners show up at your volunteer event wanting to discuss your program and how they might participate.

⮕ Secure a space large enough for the group you anticipate. If your event is in the evening, consider a fun venue like a restaurant or a bar where participants can make an evening of it by having dinner or a drink before, during, or after the event.

⮕ Advertise within your community or to a larger audience. Don't forget to include your partners! State the date, time, and location.

⮕ Recruit helpers who are familiar with the program and comfortable talking to new people.

During

⮕ Have a sign-in and information desk. This is a really good place for materials about your organization and educational handouts (and if you don't know all the attendees, a great place to collect e-mail addresses as well).

⮕ Greet people with a warm welcome and thank them for attending,

⮕ Make sure that helpers and experts are easily identified with name tags or an easy-to-spot T-shirt.

⮕ Set up the space so it is easy for potential volunteers to plug in to your organization. If you know you need help in a few categories, make signs with those topics clearly readable, and post them around the room.

⮕ Have helpers staff those stations, so they can talk with volunteers about how they can contribute to the garden.

⮕ Make clipboards, notepads, and pens available for people to sign up, write questions, or offer suggestions. Collect this material at the end of the event.

⮕ Remember, not all volunteer functions need to be garden-task related. Keep in mind that help with coordinating, managing your budget, and doing social media are valuable contributions to your garden's success. All you have to do is ask.

⮕ If your event is also to recognize volunteer contributions, provide tangible symbols of appreciation: certificates, inexpensive individualized gifts, or garden-oriented mementos.

⮕ Take photos.

After

⮕ Send a thank-you and share photos.

⮕ Solicit feedback (and volunteers) for next year.

SPRING: THE SEED SWAP

Since you're working on a food garden, vegetable seeds are a given, but what about the seeds of edible flowers or flowers that attract beneficial insects? Will you allow bulbs, onions, shallots, garlic, or Jerusalem artichokes? Do you have a policy about open-pollinated vs. hybrid seeds? Should the gardeners only bring seeds they have saved, or are commercial seeds allowed? For new gardeners, it might be easiest to just have them bring commercial seed. Many of them might be new to the concept of seeds in general and you don't want to scare them off because they haven't yet had the chance to save their own seeds.

Before

➡ Determine what the desired outcome of your seed swap should be.

➡ Secure space and check availability of convenient parking, transportation, and a place to hang coats.

➡ Determine use. You will need tables, but do you also need chairs or a seating area for older participants? Do you need a kid's area? Will there be coffee or other refreshments?

➡ Advertise the event; include date, time, and location.

➡ Let people know the rules of engagement, including what kinds of seeds are okay to bring and how much information they have to provide for seeds they may have saved that don't come with commercial packaging.

➡ Recruit helpers.

➡ Invite key garden leaders and strong volunteers to help with the mechanics of the swap and to answer any questions that might come up about the garden program.

➡ Identify expert food gardeners or seed-saving enthusiasts.

➡ Invite Master Gardeners or other garden experts in your area. (Note: Let the Master Gardeners know you're talking about food gardening. Don't assume because they are Master Gardeners they understand growing food. I know it sounds strange, but trust me on this one.)

➡ Things to consider:

Is this a chance for education on a relevant topic such as genetically engineered vs. hybrid vs. heirloom seeds?

Is this a chance to have a demonstration on seed saving or seed cleaning, or something similar?

Is this a chance to have a speaker?

Is this a chance to promote a seed company with whom you are partnering?

Is there a local seed library or community organization that would like to say a few words?

Do you want to have a raffle to raise money for your community garden?

Do you want to offer prizes, such as Seed Hoarder of the Year or Farthest Distance Traveled?

During

⇨ Provide good signage so the swap is easy to find.

⇨ Have a sign-in and information desk. This is a really good place for materials about your organization and educational handouts (and if you don't know all the swappers, it's also a good place to collect e-mail addresses).

⇨ Greet people with a warm welcome and thank them for attending.

⇨ Make sure that helpers and experts are easily identified with name tags or an easy-to-spot T-shirt.

⇨ Identify the tables (Edible Flowers! Herbs! Veggies!).

⇨ Assign someone to take pictures—your community members like to see themselves participating, and people like to be recognized.

After

⇨ Send a thank-you and share photos.

⇨ Solicit feedback (and volunteers) for next year.

⇨ Organize leftover seeds to distribute later to low-income or scholarship gardeners, or to others who may have missed the swap.

SUMMER: THE MUSIC AND GARDEN EXPERTS NIGHT

Not every area may have Master Gardeners, but I can assure you that virtually every community has garden experts. Our programs are once a month starting in July, but you can offer your programs as frequently as you can find the musicians and experts to participate. As always, when you have a group of gardeners getting together, think of it as an opportunity to speak to your members about garden management or events. You can, for example, give reminders about procedures and community rules, or make announcements for upcoming events or volunteer opportunities. On these nights, if this is the height of the season, and there's lots of ready produce, gardeners can harvest produce for donations that might go to food and nutrition programs.

Before

⇒ Publicize the details of the event.

⇒ Work with a local music school or arts group to find a performer or group whose music is in line with what your gardeners will enjoy.

⇒ Determine if the performers have or need amplification or a PA system. If they can't provide this themselves, ask your community if there is anything they can loan for the evening's event. (Small events can often be done without amplification, to avoid having to deal with sound and electricity issues.)

⇒ Identify experts to be on hand to answer garden questions, a great way to get local extension Master Gardeners involved, if your area has such a program. Master Gardeners need hours working with the public to maintain their status (number of hours varies from state to state) and this could be a great opportunity for them.

⇒ Establish and clearly identify a place for the experts to be stationed, or have them wear some identifying clothing or brightly colored hats.

During

⇒ Make sure the garden experts and the gardeners find each other and connect.

⇒ Some gardens put a tip jar out for the musicians. The musicians may want to sell CDs, so make accommodation for that possibility.

After

⇒ Clean up and thank everyone profusely.

⇒ Sign any paperwork required for the Master Gardeners to prove they participated in the program

⇒ Give the musicians anything from the tip jar and any extra produce that can be spared. "Will work for food" is especially applicable when it comes to musicians and organic veggies.

FALL: THE PLOTLUCK

Any food garden is likely to attract some avid home cooks and perhaps even professional chefs. A great way to close the loop between growing food and preparing it is to have a "plotluck" (a potluck gathering to share the fruits of your plots). Just as in a potluck meal, people bring dishes—but in this case, the food is either made from or inspired by the gardener's bounty.

Before

➡ Determine the goal of your event. Is the community at-large welcome? Should you invite your partners? What are you celebrating?

➡ Communicate event details and determine a method for deciding who brings what. A common method is assigning parts of the meal by last names.

Last names from A to F: salads, appetizers

Last names from G to L: main dishes

Last names from M to R: desserts

Last names from S to Z: drinks, ice, paper products, utensils

Of course, if someone's name falls in the salad category and they are dying to make their chocolate zucchini cake, you may have some deviation from the rules. That's okay. Another fundamental principle of plotlucks—there can never be too many desserts! If you like, encourage participants to bring recipes or talk about the idea behind their dish, particularly if any ingredients came from their own garden.

➡ Determine a few volunteers who can help with setup and cleanup.

During

➡ Have tables and seating areas set up for people to put their food out.

➡ Have small name tags and felt-tip pens so people can write what each dish is or sign their name to it.

➡ Identify where trash and recycling should go.

➡ Celebrate!

After

➡ Clean up and recycle everything.

➡ Send a thank-you and share copies of any recipes people may have brought with them.

REASONS TO CELEBRATE

You will have your own local holidays and community celebrations to look forward to. Just in case you need more excuses to get together in the garden, the following is a list of food, sustainability, and family-related events from March into December (gardening months for most areas). Maybe one of these events will resonate with your community and you can build an activity around it. If nothing else, you can share these through your communication channels as a fun FYI or learning opportunity.

MARCH

National Celery Month

National Nutrition Month—Good time to talk about and launch a nutrition garden

March 15: Ag Day—A day to celebrate our bountiful food supply

March 16: National Artichoke Hearts Day

March 22: World Water Day—A day to promote awareness about the importance of freshwater and sustainable resources

March 23: Earth Hour (8:30-9:30 p.m.)—Earth Hour encourages people to unite and take part in an event that will inspire them to reduce their environmental impact. An example of this is turning off the lights for the hour in hopes of inspiring others to be more environmentally conscious.

March 26: Spinach Day

March 31: Orange and Lemons Day

APRIL

April 6: Caesar Chavez National Day of Service

April 16: Day of the Mushroom

April 17: Healthy Kids Day

April 19: Garlic Day

April 20: Lima Bean Respect Day

April 22: Earth Day

April 23: National Picnic Day

APRIL cont.

Last Friday in April: National Arbor Day—A good time to plant a tree

Three days in April: Global Youth Service Days—Dates change every year, but this is an annual campaign that celebrates children and youth who improve their communities through service and service-learning

MAY

National Asparagus Month

National Strawberry Month

May 10: National Public Gardens Day—An annual celebration to raise awareness of public gardens and their role in environmental stewardship

May 15: International Day of Families—Created by the United Nations to encourage healthy and happy relationships within families

May 20: Pick Strawberries Day

May 28: World Hunger Day—Created by the Hunger Project to raise awareness about extreme hunger and poverty

JUNE

National Fresh Fruit and Vegetable Month

June 5: World Environment Day—A day to celebrate and encourage positive environmental action

June 10: Herb and Spices Day

June 17: National Eat Your Vegetables Day

June 18: International Picnic Day

JULY

National Culinary Arts Month

National Grilling Month

National July Belongs to Blueberries Month

July 10: Pick Blueberries Day

AUGUST

National Peach Month

August 3: National Watermelon Day

August 6: National Night Out—A night set aside for neighborhoods to gather and reinforce crime prevention, neighborhood camaraderie, and community partnerships

August 8: National Zucchini Day

August 19: Potato Day

August 22: Eat a Peach Day

Fourth Sunday in August: World Kitchen Garden Day—A day to gather with friends, family, and community members to enjoy homemade, hand-grown food

August 31: Eat Outside Day

SEPTEMBER

National Mushroom Month

National Organic Harvest Month

National Potato Month

September 7: National Acorn Squash Day

OCTOBER

National Apple Month

Vegetarian Awareness Month

October 1: World Vegetarian Day—Kickoff day for Vegetarian Awareness Month, a month to promote vegetarianism and its benefits

OCTOBER cont.

First Monday in October World Habitat Day—Created by the United Nations to encourage reflection on everyone's right to adequate shelter and to remind us about our responsibility for the future of our own habitats

October 12: World Food Day—Created by the Food and Agriculture Organization, a branch of the United Nations, to raise awareness about hunger and poverty

October 23: National Canning Day

October 24: Food Day—A nationwide U.S. celebration of more healthy, affordable, and sustainable food

October 26: Pumpkin Day

October 28: Wild Foods Day

NOVEMBER

Good Nutrition Month

National Pepper Month

Vegan Awareness Month

November 1: World Vegan Day—Kickoff day to Vegan Awareness Month, celebrating the coining of the term and the founding of The Vegan Society in November 1944

November 14: National Pickle Day

November 15: America Recycles Day—Day to educate and promote recycling throughout the United States

November 23: Eat a Cranberry Day

DECEMBER

December 1: National Pie Day

December 1: Eat a Red Apple Day

7. GROUNDWORK FOR SUCCESS

Teaching New Gardeners

Not knowing how to grow food might seem like a modern problem. Surely in the old days everyone knew how to grow their own food, right? I used to think this way, too, until I discovered that during World War II, 90 percent of the victory gardeners in Chicago had never grown anything. Zip. Nada. During the war, the city had quite a task at hand to teach food gardening to the army of food gardeners springing up overnight, needing to feed their families. And they did it very well—Chicago led the nation in the World War II victory garden movement, with 1,500 community gardens, more than 250,000 home gardens, and the largest victory garden in the United States.

Learning how to garden has not changed that much since victory gardeners met the challenge of learning to grow their own food all those years ago. According to a recent Garden Writers of America survey, friends, neighbors, or family members sharing their knowledge and skills is still the best way to learn gardening; the second most popular way is finding help and instruction through books or Internet research. Thankfully, there are many books, websites, and experts out there available to help. And the very cool thing about community gardens is that the learning is exponential. One person teaches another, and that person teaches his or her neighbors, passing along the knowledge and skills very quickly.

A challenge you may encounter when teaching in your garden is handling the many opinions on the so-called right way to garden. If you have a lot of gardeners, you may have a lot of opinions. Developing a culture of respectful sharing is essential and mutually beneficial, with everyone encouraged to voice their opinions, questions, and styles. This way people will feel free to experiment, determining on their own what works best for them.

The love of gardening is a seed once sown that never dies.

—Gertrude Jekyll

Opinions aside, there are some basic gardening principles that most people can't argue about. We will stick to those absolute fundamentals in this section so you can get your new food gardeners off to a good start. The rest of the learning comes through observation and doing, which will happen as your first season progresses and, hopefully, for years to come.

A GARDEN FRAME OF MIND

Before any instruction begins, it is important to realize that gardening isn't so much about technique but philosophy. We are a perfection-driven society; we think that if things aren't picture-perfect, we're failures. If we don't measure up to our neighbors, we're failures. If we're ten pounds overweight, we're failures. Gardening will either drive people with this mindset insane, or cure them of it. In fact, when I'm teaching gardeners, I focus on my failures most of all. If I can fail, so can they. That seems to make everything okay and allows us all to be human, fallible, and to laugh at ourselves. Then the fun can really begin.

Keep the Communication Flowing

At the Peterson Garden Project, we use our Facebook page and blog (wecangrowit.org) to provide frequent, relevant, real-time information that supports our gardeners. We also have a newsletter that we send out every two weeks in the winter; weekly in the spring, summer, and fall. We know what information to share on the blog and in the newsletter, as it's based on feedback we receive from the gardeners via our Facebook page, where gardeners post photos and ask questions or send e-mails. And, of course, we're always in the gardens, talking with folks and understanding what their current challenges are.

For gardeners who are not comfortable with computers or don't have access, we print important information on regular, letter-sized paper, slide the pages into plastic sheet protectors, and post them at the communication stations which have been set up at each garden.

One of the most important truths I've learned about community gardening is that it is a real-time, ongoing endeavor. For a program to have the biggest impact possible, you have to provide learning opportunities in a variety of ways. You can't just do a workshop at the beginning, wash the soil off your hands, and be done with teaching until next year.

Finding and Cultivating Teachers

There will be veteran gardeners and volunteers who want to lend their talents to help teach. Find these people and enlist them as resources for new gardeners. We've gone as far as placing a "green thumb" sign in expert gardeners' plots to identify them. This recognition makes the advanced gardeners proud and the new gardeners aware of fellow participants they can rely on for tried-and-true advice.

As has been mentioned, most areas also have Master Gardeners available through the local extension service. Master Gardeners are tested and certified as knowledgeable on a wide variety of garden topics and issues. They are trained to find reliable, research-based information for questions they can't answer themselves. Master Gardeners need a certain amount of hands-on teaching time annually to maintain their status and certification. Your garden might be the perfect place for them to receive the hours they need, while your gardeners receive expert help. Reach out to your local extension service to find out not only who the Master Gardeners in your area are, but also what extension classes might be offered. You don't have to provide all the education for your gardeners! Have a volunteer research what other trusted groups are doing in your area and provide this information to gardeners, so they can seek out education on their own.

Maybe the coolest thing about your garden's educational program is that today's grewbies (growing newbies!) will be tomorrow's teachers (and this is a wonderful thing to witness). During the second year of the Peterson Garden Project, one of our original grewbie gardeners, Arlene, was helping a friend get settled into her garden plot during the spring. I asked her how it was going and she told me what she was showing her friend. And, she proudly announced, "I just told her—relax! Stuff wants to grow!" I was impressed and said so—then she said, "LaManda, don't you remember? You told me that last year!" It was true. And that was the very advice I had gotten from my father when he was teaching me as a child. My conversation with Arlene always makes me smile.

Education throughout the Growing Season

The Peterson Garden Project was set up as an education program to teach people how to grow their own food. And our gardens are big—often with 500 to 800 people participating in each. So, clearly, one-on-one instruction is almost impossible (note the "almost"). To get the biggest impact out of limited volunteer resources, we've had to be smart about how we provide education. Regardless of the size of your garden, you'll need to prepare for educational instruction throughout the growing season—not just in the spring. And you'll need to adapt

KNOW YOUR ZONE FOR SUCCESSFUL GARDENING

No matter where we are gardening in the world, we are all impacted by the weather. Each garden is subject to the seasons and the unique elements of climate.

Gardening is a very local endeavor, and this aspect is essential for you and your gardeners to understand when thinking about the plants and techniques that will make your garden succeed. Because growing conditions can be so different, it is somewhat futile for a gardener in North Dakota to read a book about gardening in California. This awareness of regional differences is a basic fact that your gardeners need to comprehend.

While it may take years to fully understand the unique factors of your local climate, it's useful to start with identifying the bookends of the garden season: the frost dates.

Average frost dates can help you calculate when to plant cool-season crops, when to start seeds inside, when you can plant hot crops (peppers, eggplant, tomatoes) without fear of killing or stunting young plants, when you should plant succession crops (a second planting of crops that will do better in cool, fall weather), when you should plan on taking your garden down (ending the growing season), or when to begin planning a winter garden (perhaps with some root crops or sturdy greens like kale).

Each region of the world publishes a resource for determining frost dates. In the United States, it is the United States Department of Agriculture (USDA) hardiness zone map. For an interactive version of the USDA hardiness zone map, go to usna.usda.gov/Hardzone/ushzmap.html. Plant hardiness data for Canada can be found at planthardiness.gc.ca/. Or visit atlas.nrcan.gc.ca/site/english/maps/environment/forest/forestcanada/planthardi. For Europe, go to gardenweb.com/zones/europe/ or uk.gardenweb.com/forums/zones/hze.html. For hardiness ratings for the UK with USDA equivalents, visit rhs.org.uk/Plants/Plant-trials-and-awards/pdf/2012_RHS-Hardiness-Rating.

to the needs of the community, while using the resources you've got available. It is sometimes a fine balance, being able to provide the right education at the right time, but with a little practice, you'll figure out what your gardeners need to know and how to share the best information in a way that is most helpful.

Teaching Basic Garden Skills

Developing a very basic instructional program—enough to get new gardeners settled at the start of the season without overwhelming them with too much information—is the best approach. I can't stress how important this is! Beginners can be easily discouraged, so it is good to dispense information as needed and in a variety of ways to make the learning relevant and powerful. You'll be able to tailor the educational offerings as the garden grows and as teaching resources become available; needs change throughout the season, and skills become relevant as the garden season unfolds. The garden is a living classroom.

What follows is a suggestion for a simple set of skills-building workshops or instructional sessions for your gardeners, based on the seasons—from planning, through planting, maintenance, harvest, and season wrap-up. This basic approach is a good start for new gardeners:

winter planning will teach skills required to get your participants thinking logically about their garden's design; hands-on spring workshops will get gardeners in and settled; summer skills can be provided as learning opportunities present themselves naturally as the season progresses; and fall sessions can focus on winding down the active phase of growing food.

WINTER—PLANNING THE GARDEN

To keep the garden community active year-round, we encourage gardeners to acquire skills early and to use the cold winter months for planning. This is particularly beneficial for brand-new gardeners.

We suggest that gardeners use a free, simple online garden planning tool; these can be found at many gardening websites. These nifty aids allow gardeners to not only plan their garden with a simple user interface, they usually provides planting advice customized to the garden that's just been planned. Typically, multiple garden designs can be saved so new gardeners have lots of opportunities to dream and design. This self-directed learning experience is a great way for new gardeners to become comfortable with the garden design and crop selection processes. And, since it is a self-paced exercise, people can do it when it is most convenient to have computer access; not all of your gardeners are going to have computers or be computer-savvy, but many will. Encourage those with the know-how to reach out to others who might need a little computer assistance.

Winter Education Topics

➡ Working with the Sun

➡ Making the Most of Small Spaces

➡ Planning for Plant-Growth Needs

➡ Annuals vs. Perennials

➡ Row or Intensive Plant Spacing

WORKING WITH THE SUN

When you picked a community garden site, it's likely that you chose the best possible location for maximum sun exposure, but there are times—due to trees, buildings, or other obstructions—when all areas of the community garden will not get full coverage. It is important to make gardeners aware of crops that can work in the conditions specific to their plot location. And, sometimes, it takes a season in the garden to see the light patterns and how they impact a particular area. If a bed is in a potentially shady spot, this information will be useful to new gardeners, so they don't get discouraged when they can't grow their prized, sun-loving crop. Many popular garden vegetables, like tomatoes and peppers, need 6 to 8 hours of full sun to reach maturity. But there are lots of other crops that can grow successfully with limited sun.

Location, Location, Location

Crops for Part Sun (2 to 4 hours)	Crops for Dappled Sun
Chives	Beet greens
Cilantro	Cabbage (small headed varieties)
Leafy greens	Endive
Parsley	Leeks
Peas	Lettuce
Scallions	Radishes
	Spinach
	Turnip greens

Plan your garden to take best advantage of available sun year-round.

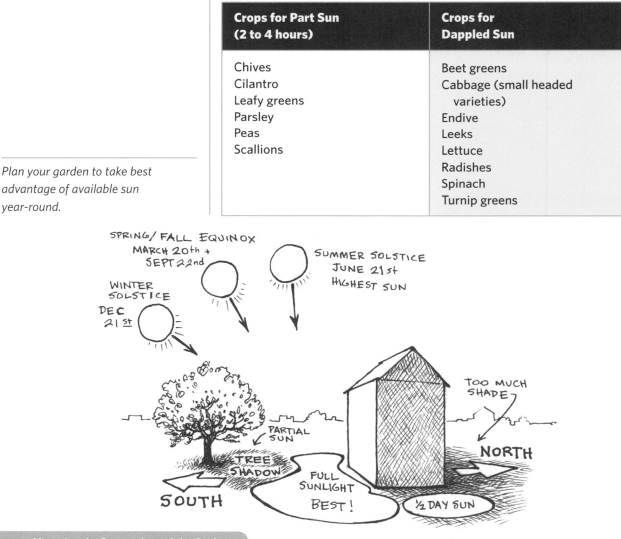

SPRING/ FALL EQUINOX MARCH 20th + SEPT 22nd

SUMMER SOLSTICE JUNE 21st HIGHEST SUN

WINTER SOLSTICE DEC 21st

TOO MUCH SHADE

NORTH

PARTIAL SUN

TREE SHADOW

FULL SUNLIGHT BEST!

½ DAY SUN

SOUTH

Depending on the layout of your community garden, individual gardeners may or may not have endless room to plant everything they want to grow. Particularly with individual raised-bed allotment gardens, gardeners need to be selective about planting space-hogging crops like squash, melons, and pumpkins. They'll grow rapidly and produce creeping vines that can easily take over a small space.

Is it really worth it to grow a watermelon in a small space? Your gardeners will have to decide for themselves. If they're growing food to save money, a crop's value can be measured in terms of price per pound, keeping in mind that vegetable prices vary depending on region, season, and where they shop. It is also possible to determine value by how much a crop yields relative to the space it takes up. Of course, taste buds and sentiment might win out over economics. It's always okay to grow something for the sheer joy of growing it. So even though potatoes may be cheaper to buy than to grow, they're sure fun to dig up, come harvest time!

Value of Crops

More Bang for the Buck High value for the amount of space a plant takes up—typically cheaper to grow than buy.	Less Bang for the Buck Low value for the amount of space a plant takes up—typically cheaper to buy than grow.
Arugula	Broccoli
Asparagus	Cabbage
Basil	Cauliflower
Beans	Corn
Beets	Melons
Cucumbers	Potatoes
Eggplant	Pumpkins
Kale	Winter squash
Lettuce	
Mint	
Onions	
Parsley	
Peppers	
Radishes	
Rhubarb	
Scallions	
Summer squash	
Swiss chard	
Tomatoes	
Turnips	
Zucchini	

PLANNING FOR PLANT-GROWTH NEEDS

Your new gardeners may not understand how big plants can get while they're growing, or how they look when fully grown. Vegetable size doesn't necessarily correspond to the size of a parent plant. For instance, okra pods are quite small, but an okra plant can grow over 4 feet tall and 3 feet wide.

It is good to educate gardeners on the size of a plant and the direction of the sunlight. A spatial understanding is valuable, so that larger crops don't shadow smaller crops or make the smaller plants inaccessible. This is particularly important with raised bed gardening, where your gardeners will be reaching in from the perimeter to tend plants in the middle. It can also be important in a tightly packed urban community garden—you don't want someone's giant sunflowers casting a four-hour shadow on a neighbor's plot.

Plant Sizes at Full Maturity

Small	Medium	Large
Beets	Basil	Beans
Carrots	Collards	Broccoli
Chives	Eggplant	Brussels sprouts
Cilantro	Kale	Cabbage
Endive	Lavender	Cauliflower
Garlic	Oregano	Corn
Leeks	Peppers (hot)	Cucumbers
Lettuce	Rosemary	Melons
Onions	Sage	Okra
Parsley	Swiss chard	Peas
Parsnips		Peppers (bell, poblano)
Radishes		Potatoes
Spinach		Pumpkins
Turnips		Summer squash
		Sunflowers
		Tomatillos
		Tomatoes
		Winter squash
		Zucchini

Most vegetables are annuals, which means that they complete their life cycle in one season and require replanting every year from seeds or seedlings. However, a few vegetables, and many herbs and fruits, are perennials. The plants die back in the fall, sprouting up again in the spring on their own, depending on where you live and the cold hardiness of the plant. Edible perennials are a worthwhile investment. Favorites such as rhubarb and asparagus take a couple of seasons to establish themselves, but can produce for many years. Perennials will need a permanent location, or maybe even a bed of their own. Your gardeners should be aware of the year-to-year benefits of perennials. When there is space and interest, a shared bed of favorites like rhubarb or blueberries can be installed as a community project.

ANNUALS VS. PERENNIALS

Perennial Food Plants

Asparagus
Blackberries
Blueberries
Bunching onions
Chives
Jerusalem artichokes
    (sunchokes)
Lavender
Mint
Raspberries
Rhubarb
Sage
Sorrel
Strawberries

There are a number of planting schemes and methods out there. For the sake of simplicity, we're going to focus on two methods: row gardening (or, as I like to call it, farm gardening) and intensive gardening (which utilizes elements of the square-foot gardening method pioneered by Mel Bartholomew in the 1970s).

Row gardening is the method most beginners think of when they think of gardening. Picture an old-school farm with long, straight rows of assorted crops: a row of corn, a row of turnips, a row of cucumbers, and so on. Row gardening will work really well if your community garden is set up with, well, long rows—and lots of them. Many food-pantry gardens are set up this way for maximum yield. For row gardening, you can pretty much follow seed-package instructions (in terms of planting, spacing, and thinning) and go to town.

Row gardening gets a little tricky in smaller spaces, raised beds, and allotment gardens. With limited real estate, gardeners generally want a variety of crops in their limited space, and this is where intensive gardening can be helpful. Intensive gardening segments off the growing space into square-foot sections; each section is sown with a different crop. Some expertise is required to determine where plants

ROW OR INTENSIVE PLANT SPACING

are best placed (so as to not shadow other crops or make it impossible to reach the middle of the bed). But, generally speaking, intensive gardening is an excellent, easy method for most new gardeners to embrace.

From a planting standpoint, row gardening is pretty simple: pick a crop and plant it in a straight row. Things can be slightly more complicated in a raised-bed environment; but once gardeners become familiar with plant sizes, they'll be able to plan a raised-bed layout. The intensive gardening technique divides the bed into a grid, with each square measuring a square foot. Plantings are organized per square foot. So if you have 12 square feet, you'll have 12 squares in which to plant.

But your gardeners won't necessarily have 12 plants—in fact, they will have many more. Plant spacing is determined by mature plant size, which varies widely. Cabbage and tomato plants, for example, are large and should be allotted one square foot each, at minimum. On the other hand, beets and spinach are small and can be planted up to 9 per square foot.

When situating plants, visualize them in three dimensions as they grow up and out. A cabbage plant might grow 1 to 2 feet wide, but stay compact and low lying, measuring only 6 to 18 inches tall. In contrast, a tomato plant could grow many feet in height and sprawl outward, potentially shading nearby plants (spinach might benefit from this shade, but your beets will need full sun). Consider the growth habit and sun requirements of each plant, and plan accordingly.

Here's a table that shows how to convert row spacing from a seed package to intensive spacing. The primary difference between row and intensive gardening is in the spacing and configuration of plantings. Traditionally, seed packages suggest spacing for row gardening as "plant in row, thin to 2 inches between plants." With intensive gardening, you'll plant the seeds where you want them to go in the first place, and thinning is not required.

Seed Spacing for Intensive Gardening

Spacing recommended on seed packets (row planting)	12 inches		6 inches		4 inches		3 inches	
Number of seeds to plant per square foot (intensive planting)	1 seed	•	4 seeds	::	9 seeds	⋮⋮⋮	16 seeds	::::

SPRING—PLANTING THE GARDEN

At the beginning of the season (for Chicago this means mid-April) we have a series of workshops in each of the gardens for new gardeners. These one-hour sessions are meant only to get their 4-by-8 plot planted with confidence. They're very basic, but they're enough to get new gardeners settled. Dispense information as it is needed throughout the season to make the learning relevant and "sticky."

Spring Education Topics

➡ Understanding Healthy Soil and Organic Gardening

➡ Seeds and How to Plant Them

➡ Choosing Seeds vs. Seedlings

➡ How to Plant a Tomato Seedling

➡ How to Plant Other Seedlings

➡ How to Water Properly

THINK ABOUT THE KITCHEN WHEN YOU'RE THINKING ABOUT THE GARDEN

Picking what to grow can be intimidating and overwhelming, with the seed catalogs full of so many options. I encourage first-year gardeners to grow what they want to eat. Sure, they might want to experiment with something exotic, but I suggest that they start with the basics, branching out to new things once the first year is under their belt. This doesn't mean they can't get creative! We had a new gardener one season who loved the color purple. She picked her favorite foods, choosing varieties that bore purple produce—beans, tomatoes, eggplant— for a lovely garden!

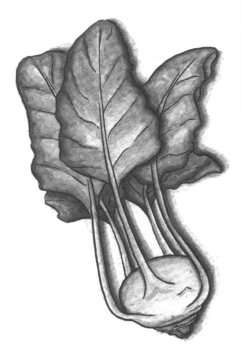

UNDERSTANDING HEALTHY SOIL AND ORGANIC GARDENING

ORGANIC GARDENING

At Peterson Garden Project, we are proponents of organic gardening and teach only this method. If your garden isn't organic, it isn't the end of the world (and we'll still love you), but I would encourage you to consider organic methods for your garden if your situation allows.

So what exactly is organic gardening? It's a practice that supports the long-term health of soil, plants, ecosystems, and people. It means working with nature, conserving garden resources, and promoting biodiversity, or variety, in all forms of life—plants, animals, and microorganisms. The more variety and the healthier the ecosystem, the greater the garden's chances of success.

Organic gardening means you do not use any synthetic chemicals or fertilizers. You also use non-toxic prevention methods with pests and diseases. Using chemical pesticides kills all bugs—good and bad. An organic garden works to encourage beneficial insects, which in turn prey on the bad bugs. Chemicals in the garden prevent this from happening. There is also an ongoing concern about the long-term effects on humans from exposure to chemicals.

Good soil is the foundation of a healthy garden, and the care of the soil is the most important job for an organic gardener. If this is your first year with your new food garden, you will most likely be in good shape with healthy, fresh soil. But, moving forward, it is important for your gardeners to know that the less they tinker with the soil, the more fertile it will be. Millions of organisms, such as earthworms, fungi, algae, and microscopic bacteria are at work in healthy soil, creating, storing, and distributing essential nutrients. Your gardeners can protect and help nurture these creatures by minimizing soil disturbances. Many gardeners, especially in the spring, get excited and want to turn the soil. Avoid this—especially in raised beds—as it can disrupt the complex, balanced ecosystem that's already in place, resulting in soil degradation. Also, discourage your gardeners from walking on the soil, which will compact and collapse air pockets needed to move water and oxygen to plants.

COMPOST

To build and maintain healthy soil after your first year, you'll need to add organic matter on a regular basis. Compost is organic matter also known as black gold, made up of vegetable scraps, yard waste, and manure that has decomposed over a period of weeks or months, breaking down into a crumbly soil-like texture. Adding compost to the soil replenishes nutrients, improves the soil's ability to hold air and water, and promotes good drainage. Compost serves as food and nourishment for all the organisms in your soil. It's the most essential ingredient in organic soil.

As you build your garden program, be sure to think about how gardeners can add compost to their plots. Is this a program you'll offer through on-site composting, or will they be encouraged to bring their own amendments? If so, how often? Work with a team of volunteer experts to determine a soil health plan, and share it with your gardeners so they can be stewards of the soil, too.

Soil will stay fertile and won't require chemical or synthetic fertilizers, so long as it is nurtured. And the healthier the soil, the less likely your gardeners are to encounter pests and disease in the garden. Still, unwanted guests might pay a visit from time to time. Organic approaches to pest and disease management are effective alternatives to using pesticides and herbicides that can kill good organisms as well as bad ones.

Crop diversity—that is, growing the greatest variety of plants possible—helps create and sustain a healthy garden ecosystem. Each plant (non-edibles included) creates habitat and food for different creatures. The more varieties grown, the more opportunities for complex interactions to take place. In a community garden, this variety seems to happen naturally. As many families grow their own combination of annuals, perennials, and non-edibles, there's plenty of variety to help support a good ecosystem and healthy pollinator populations.

OMRI: ORGANIC MATERIALS REVIEW INSTITUTE

When you're working with many people, standards are a good thing. You can't be with all of your gardeners when they're shopping for fertilizers or mulch or pest control. Make your gardeners aware of what to look for by encouraging them to check for the OMRI label. This means the product has been reviewed by the Organic Materials Review Institute, ensuring compliance with USDA organic standards. Your gardeners need not choose OMRI products exclusively; this is merely a way to help them make informed choices. You can also check for OMRI-listed products online at www.omri.org.

SEEDS AND HOW TO PLANT THEM

Seeds, like soil, are a foundation of the vegetable garden—and seed varieties abound. There's often confusion about which varieties are best and what the terms surrounding them really mean. GMO hybrid, or heirloom, seeds don't make any sense unless your gardeners have a basic understanding of these and other terms before they set out to buy seeds. Many gardeners are confused (and sometimes scared) about the differences between seeds and their crops. This information is good to share with them in the spring, when they are shopping for seeds, which also provides an opportunity to connect with the gardeners during the winter months.

The terms GE (genetically engineered) and GMO (genetically modified organism) are often used interchangeably, but do not mean the same thing. Genetic engineering is the scientific practice of incorporating genes directly into an organism by way of recombinant DNA techniques. GE plants do not occur in nature, but are a product of human intervention. GE seeds cannot be purchased in consumer seed catalogs or garden centers. Presently GE techniques are used only in large-scale agriculture, and are the subject of ongoing ethical debate.

A GMO is an organism produced by any means of genetic modification, whether by modern genetic engineering or age-old plant-breeding methods. For thousands of years, plant breeders have manipulated organisms to improve quality and productivity, making the same kinds of selections that could, technically, also occur naturally. Seedless watermelon and plucots are examples of modern GMOs.

A hybrid is created when a breeder cross-pollinates two pure plant lines to produce a seed with desirable traits—such as disease resistance, uniformity, or color—from both parents. Popular home garden hybrids include 'Sungold' and 'Better Boy' tomatoes. Production methods for hybrids are highly controlled and must remain consistent from one year to the next. Seeds can be saved and planted from hybrids, but there's no guarantee that plants grown from these seeds will contain the desirable characteristics of the parent plants.

On the other hand, seeds that are saved from open-pollinated varieties and then planted in subsequent years will produce plants with the same characteristics of the parent plant. Open pollination occurs naturally, without human intervention, via insects, wind, or self-pollination (when both male and female flowers reside on the same plant). The term heirloom describes any open-pollinated variety existing prior to the 1940s and '50s, when plant breeders began producing modern hybrids. As the name suggests, many heirloom varieties have been passed down through generations of gardeners. Heirloom seeds, like hybrid seeds, are grown on a commercial scale and sold to seed distribution companies.

Any seed packet labeled Certified Organic has been produced in strict accordance with the USDA's National Organic Program. Organic seeds are grown without the use of synthetic fertilizers and pesticides, sewage sludge, irradiation, or genetic engineering. In addition, the land on which organic crops are grown cannot have had prohibited substances applied for three years prior to harvest.

Do you have to buy organic seeds? No. When it comes to organic gardening, how plants are grown matters more than using organic seeds. Organizations that grow organic seeds are doing good work and need support. But if that special variety your gardeners want is only available as a conventionally raised seed, encourage them to get it!

SEEDS TO SHARE

Most seed packets contain more than enough seeds for one season. Let your gardeners know that they don't have to feel obligated to plant a whole packet at one time. Encourage them to plant only what's needed, saving the rest of the seeds for next year or to share with gardening neighbors.

Seeds can last up to five years if stored properly. It is best to store them in their original packet, inside an airtight container, away from warmth and humidity (avoiding humidity is more important than avoiding heat). Germination rates of stored seeds will gradually decrease over time, but gardeners can compensate for this by planting a few seeds instead of just one to ensure that at least one seed will sprout.

Seed Lifespans for Popular Plants

Popular Plants	Years Seeds Can Be Stored
Corn, onions	1–2
Chives, okra, parsley	2–3
Beans, carrots, peas	3–4
Beets, peppers, Swiss chard, tomatoes	4–5
Basil, broccoli, cabbage, cauliflower, cucumber, eggplant, lettuce, melon, radish, spinach, squash	5–6

SEED PACKAGE TERMINOLOGY

Your gardeners may see some unfamiliar terminology as they're reading seed and plant labels—specifically for beans, squash, and tomatoes. The terms bush, vine, determinate, and indeterminate describe the growth habit of these plants. Understanding what these terms mean will affect which varieties they buy, where they choose to locate the plants in their growing areas, and what devices they use to support the plants—so be sure to dedicate time in this workshop to making sure that gardeners understand these terms.

A bush variety is **determinate**, meaning that it will grow to a certain size and then stop growing, at which point it will flower and bear all of its fruit within a few weeks. A vine variety is **indeterminate**, meaning that it will continue growing and producing fruit throughout the entire season, until the first frost. Bush varieties grow lower to the ground (about 3 to 5 feet) and require minimal physical support, while vine varieties can grow quite long (up to 10 or even 15 feet) and need to be trellised in order to thrive and be productive.

Gardeners will also run into the term "pole" when shopping for beans. Pole beans are a vine variety, as opposed to bush beans, which are low, self-supporting plants. Pole beans need support and can get quite unruly, so, in a small-space garden, bush varieties might be a better choice.

In most cases, winter squash (such as butternut and acorn) are indeterminate in their growth habit. Summer squash (such as zucchini and yellow crookneck) are usually determinate and have a bush habit. Even so, summer squash plants are not small. In fact, they tend to be space hogs and often grow wider than they are tall. These are important considerations in a small-space garden, where a gangly plant can encroach on neighbors or crowd out other plantings.

WHEN TO PLANT SEEDS

Once you've determined your growing climate by looking up your USDA hardiness zone (or whatever resource is commonly used where you live), you'll understand the frost bookends for your garden season. The accompanying table gives you the guidelines for what can survive best in various temperatures.

Planting Crops by Temperature

	Cool Season: Spring and Fall	Hot Season: Summer
Required soil temperature for seed germination	45–55 degrees F	55–65 degrees F
Required air temperature for plant growth	40–60 degrees F	60 degrees F or above
Recommended crops	Beets Broccoli Brussels sprouts Cabbage Carrots Cauliflower Celery Chives Kohlrabi Lavender Leafy greens Onions Parsley Parsnips Peas Potatoes Radishes Turnips	Basil Beans Corn Cucumbers Eggplant Melons Okra Peppers Summer squash Sweet potatoes Tomatoes Winter squash Zucchini

How deep to plant seeds

Teaching your gardeners how deeply to plant seeds is essential. If I've seen it once, I've seen it a hundred times: given no instruction, brand-new gardeners will jam seeds into the ground as far as their fingers will reach. Then they'll be really sad when nothing comes up. Trust me on this. So be sure to emphasize this critical information: seeds need to be planted at the *proper* depth. In general, plant 2 to

LABELING CROPS

An unmarked plant isn't the end of the world; your gardeners will probably figure out what it is eventually (although this can create an unfortunate situation with unidentified hot peppers). But since we want to create an army of well-trained gardeners, it is very important to share the following with your newbies. Especially the part about permanent markers!

As plants begin to sprout, they can look very similar to one another—especially if multiple varieties of a certain vegetable are planted ("I think that's leaf lettuce. Wait . . . no, it's romaine!"). So you'll want to be able to tell your plants apart when they start to mature and have more defining characteristics. But until then, mark seeds or seedlings when you put them in the ground, using the plastic inserts from their original pots if they were purchased at a nursery. This helps avoid confusion. To mark seeds or seedlings that don't have tags, you can use markers made from Popsicle sticks, paint stirring sticks, cut-up mini-blinds, or broken terra-cotta pot shards. Be creative (this is a fun way to get kids involved). Whatever markers you use, just make sure to label them with a permanent marker so the ink won't wash off in the rain or fade due to sun exposure.

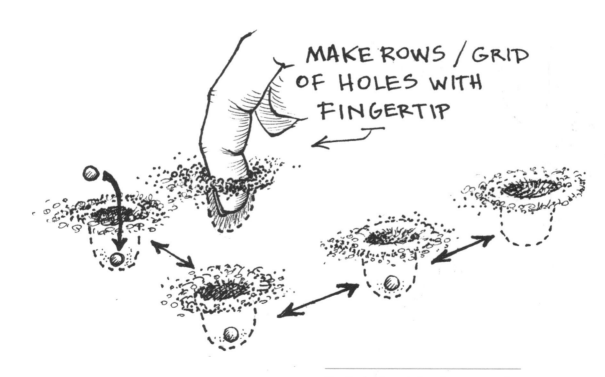

Don't plant seeds too deep; generally 2 to 4 times as deep as the seed's thickness.

4 times as deep as the seed's thickness. For large seeds, like peas, poke holes in the soil with your finger to the proper depth, insert the seeds, and cover them lightly with soil. Smaller seeds are planted closer to the soil's surface, taking care not to push them in too deep or they won't germinate.

Seeds for lettuce and other salad greens are quite small, and separating them can be tricky, if not impossible. Go ahead and plant these seeds in small groupings, or pinches, to ensure that at least one germinates. If all of your seeds end up germinating, then you'll see a few seedlings sprouting up in a cluster. Once the seedlings are a few inches tall, you can thin them by removing the extras and leaving the biggest, healthiest-looking one intact so that it continues to grow. Trim the extra seedlings at soil level with scissors or garden shears. Pulling them by hand disturbs the roots of the remaining seedling. If you have a lot of these trimmings, you can eat them; in the grocery store they're very expensive and called "micro greens"!

Another approach to planting leafy greens (usually not printed on the seed packet) is to broadcast, or sprinkle, them over an area (as if you're adding salt to a dish), and then cover them with a very thin layer of soil. Instead of removing extra seedlings, let them continue to grow and then harvest their outer leaves every so often for a salad of baby greens. By cutting only a few leaves at a time from each plant, the plants will stay alive and continue producing. This method of growing is referred to as "cut and come again."

"CUT AND COME AGAIN" GREENS – CLIPPING

EAT!

LET INNER STALKS GROW MORE.

CUT OUTER STALKS ONLY

EAT!

CUT NEAR BASE.

USE CLIPPERS DO NOT TEAR OFF!

CHOOSING SEEDS VS. SEEDLINGS

Seeds vary in terms of how long they take to germinate (sprout) and grow into mature plants. For instance, radishes typically take 4 weeks to grow from seed to harvest. In contrast, tomatoes take about 17 weeks, and eggplants and peppers take 19 weeks. While your gardeners can start any crop from seeds planted directly in the ground, for crops that mature slowly such as tomatoes, eggplants and peppers, I suggest purchasing seedlings (young plants) from a local nursery and transplanting them into their gardens.

As an alternative to buying seedlings from a local nursery, many new gardeners are excited about growing plants from seed. Seed starting is not a difficult project, per se. The trouble comes with the lighting available to nurture the plant from seed to young transplant. Often the light in a sunny window isn't enough to get the plants off to a robust start; these seedlings will grow spindly or be disease prone. Lovingly tended plants that end up with these conditions will be a real downer for the rookie gardener. This is why I recommend buying transplants the first year. Once gardeners get a season under their belt, they'll be used to how plants grow and how healthy plants behave. Then they can tackle seed starting. Teachers can perhaps work with a group for a late-winter activity—another opportunity to bring your community together. If you have access to a communal greenhouse or hoop house, then forget what I just said. Let them start their seeds right from the get-go and enjoy the fun.

Direct-Seeded Crops

Life Cycle for Popular Direct-Seeded Crops	Average Weeks to Maturity (from seed to harvest)
Cress, mustard greens, radishes	4–5
Arugula, beans (bush), beets, lettuce, Swiss chard, tatsoi	6–8
Endive, kale, spinach, summer squash	7–8
Cucumbers, peas	8–10
Corn	9–13
Beans (pole), carrots, peas, turnips	10
Basil, melon, okra, winter squash	12
Cauliflower, parsley	14
Broccoli, cabbage, chives	16

Another key task you'll need to teach your gardeners is the distinction between how to plant a seedling and how to plant a *tomato* seedling—because the process is different.

Some gardeners spend their lives trying to figure out the secret to growing great tomatoes, and there are a lot of passionate opinions on the topic. While there's no simple answer, I think a good place to start is with a strong root system, which means planting tomatoes differently than you would other seedlings.

Tomatoes can develop roots all along their stems, so burying a large portion of the stem when you put it in the ground will increase the size of the root system—and the tomato plants will need less water, be better at withstanding summer storms, and will likely yield more fruit.

To plant the tomato seedling, begin by first digging a shallow trench—almost as long as the seedling is tall. Trim off the leaves from the lower portion of the stem (this is the part to bury). Remove the seedling from its pot and loosen the root ball, then lay it horizontally into the trench. Fill the trench with soil and gently bend the stem upward (don't worry—it will straighten up as it grows). Give the plant water right away after planting to avoid transplant shock, and then water it frequently (daily if possible) for the first week or so, until it's settled into its new home.

It is important for new gardeners to understand that this process is only applicable to tomatoes. Otherwise they could end up killing all the other seedlings in their garden, which would be a disappointment.

HOW TO PLANT A TOMATO SEEDLING

Remove leaves from lower part of stem and lay plant horizontally at the bottom of the trench.

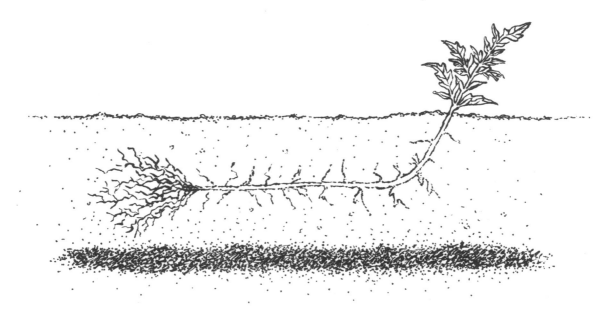

HOW TO PLANT OTHER SEEDLINGS

If you're starting from a young plant, or seedling, rather than a seed, the transplanting process is pretty straightforward. First make sure the plant is well watered. Dig a hole in the soil that is the same height as the plant's root ball, and just wide enough to fit the root ball without forcing or squishing it. Then remove the plant from its pot and gently loosen the bottom of the root ball.

Now place the seedling into the hole so that it stands straight up; the top of the plant should be at the same level as the soil (you do not want soil covering the stem), then lightly spread the soil back around the stem for support. Build a saucer-shaped depression into the soil around the plant's base to help direct water toward the roots. Then water it immediately at the base. The plant may droop at first (a new habitat can be a bit of a shock), but with regular watering, it should perk up within a couple days.

STAGGERED PLANTINGS

I find that most new gardeners, especially small-space gardeners, are a little overwhelmed by the idea of staggered planting, as they've just begun wrapping their heads around the absolute basics. But after a season of paying attention to how things grow—and noticing that they had an overabundance of their favorite vegetables all at once—they should find this method makes a lot more sense.

Staggered planting follows the same rules and techniques as any other type of planting, except that you make a conscious effort to sow a succession of seeds weekly, so your harvest is spread out. It does require a little planning in terms of how you use your space—as one square is starting to sprout, others may be empty or just germinating with new seeds.

Good Crops for Staggered Plantings

Beans (bush)
Beets
Carrots
Lettuce
Peas
Radishes
Spinach
Swiss chard

DEALING WITH ROOT-BOUND PLANTS

Matted roots around the outside of the root ball mean the plant has become root-bound, due to the constraints of growing in a pot. Not to worry—the roots can be loosened by teasing them gently out of their circling pattern. Tug just the outer roots and leave the core ones intact. It's okay if there's a little pop or crack (you're not traumatizing the plant, but encouraging its roots to grow outward). If the roots can't be loosened easily, run a knife along the exterior or bottom of the root ball wherever the matting has occurred, or gently (*gently!*) "crack" the bottom of the root ball by pulling it apart until you hear the roots breaking apart.

Teaching new gardeners how to water properly is another essential task—maybe one of the *most* essential. And here's an observation from the garden trenches: there are people who love to water—*love* to water—and they will happily stand around spraying everything they can reach. We've actually had to ask some people to not water other peoples' gardens (I personally hate watering and would welcome this!) because the gardeners wanted to do it themselves—and rightly so, understanding the importance of watering to a successful garden.

Watering during the seed germination period is really important. If you're lucky, it rains and nature does the work for you. If not, then you'll need to make sure your soil stays moist in order for the seeds to germinate. This might mean watering every day if the weather is dry. You don't need to soak the soil—just keep it damp by using a watering can with a rose (a round disk perforated with tiny holes that screws onto the watering can stem), a spray bottle that mists, or the fan or mist setting on your hose's spray nozzle (staying aware that if you use a forceful setting, you might end up washing all the seeds into a corner—*oops!*).

Continue watering every day after the seeds have sprouted, since they don't have an established root system yet and can dry out quickly. At this point, you can start watering gently around the base of the seedlings. After the plants have grown an inch or two, you can let them dry out a little between waterings.

HOW TO WATER PROPERLY

Watering can make or break a plant's chances for success.

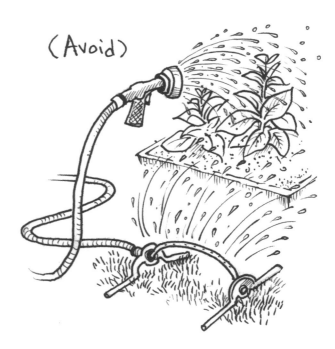

Water at base!

(Avoid)

KIDS **LOVE** TO WATER

Often children are overlooked as volunteers, which is unfortunate because I've never seen a child who doesn't like actively participating in their community garden. Children are great instructors for simple tasks like watering. So, early in the season, we get all the children under age 10 together (some of the older ones hang out on the periphery, picking their nails and pretending not to care) and appoint them to be Water Ambassadors. This includes a few key assignments:

➡ Make sure everyone is watering properly at the base of the plant.

➡ Make sure nobody is wasting water by leaving the faucets running.

➡ Make sure water is turned off when they leave the garden.

Easy stuff, right? You'd think you'd given them keys to their parents' cars. Kids love having a job to do in the garden; and it is hysterical to see a 5-year-old talking to a grown-up, giving instructions on water conservation or proper watering techniques. Even more hysterical is that the adults listen! Everyone has a job to do in the garden. Give kids this important task and proper watering will be the least of your concerns.

Once the plants are established, the best way to water is by hand, or positioning a hose nozzle close to the base of the plant. Overhead watering methods like sprinklers are fine for lawns and shrubs, but not for vegetables. Excessive moisture on leaves can harbor fungal diseases; and if an infected plant is watered from above or the side, the disease can spread to other nearby plants. Emphasize to your gardeners that plants need water sent to their roots.

WATER WORRIES

More than almost anything else, not watering at the appropriate time (or at all) will kill plants. Many gardeners, particularly first-timers, may not realize the commitment that watering their plot involves. Vacations and other summer happenings can get in the way of people regularly tending and watering their beds, and this can create worry and frustration, both for the gardeners themselves and for other gardeners who are watching lovely produce die on the vine for lack of care.

To solve this problem in the Peterson Garden Project gardens, we created "water me" sticks. Gardeners who were going to be out of town could place the stick in their plot to signal to other gardeners that they needed assistance. We found that there were some people who loved to water and would make an effort to find the "water me" sticks and tend those plots—no matter how far away from their own bed. When the gardeners returned from vacation, the sticks went back to the storage area for others to use. We have several on hand in each garden and the system really works.

As with anything, you'll find the one person who puts a "water me" stick in their bed at the start of the summer and would leave it there all season if someone didn't remove it. Make the rules clear about the system, and it can go a long way toward a healthy, happy garden with participants who help each other with this critical task.

SUMMER—WHAT'S HAPPENING IN THE GARDEN

The spring busy season is over, you've taught the basics, and hopefully everything is growing strong. Life in the garden slows down to a more manageable pace as people water, tend their germinating seeds and seedlings, and await the first big harvests of high summer. To help gardeners along their way, this is the time to share the next round of skills.

These topics address what gardeners will most likely encounter during the height of the growing season. In our gardens, they are hands-on sessions taught by volunteer Master Gardeners. You can offer them throughout the summer (and beyond; we schedule them June to October) because they are relevant to what's happening in garden plots as the season progresses.

Summer Education Topics

➡ How to Trellis Plants

➡ Recognizing and Dealing with Pests and Plant Diseases

➡ The Weed Walk: How to Recognize Weeds

HOW TO TRELLIS PLANTS

*As vertical crops mature, they'll need support to keep from sprawl-*ing out of control. It's easiest to install such structures early on, when plants are small; waiting until later might disturb plant roots. A small cage, trellis, or stakes should be sufficient for most determinate plants. Plants that vine continuously—such as pole beans, winter squash, and melons—will need a taller, wider trellis system.

Vertical crops will need varying levels of attention throughout the season, depending on their climbing habit. Beans are self-climbers, so they'll do fine on their own as long as they have a trellis to climb. Cucumbers, winter squash, and melons will wrap their tendrils around nearby supports. Secure the vines to supports with flexible garden tape, twist ties, or rope (try not to tear the tendrils as you do this—gently unwind them if necessary, and then wrap them back around the supports). Gardeners can let them go and the plants will find their way, or vines can be trained, which will help plants grow in a preferred direction.

Trellises support vertical growth, which saves space.

SUPPORTING TOMATOES

Regardless of what tomato varieties your gardeners choose, the plants will need some form of physical support as they grow. Particularly in allotment gardens, where every square inch of ground is precious, keeping tomatoes growing up makes everything easier.

Tomato support structures—commonly referred to as cages—come in many styles, including square, round, conical, and ladder-shaped. They cost anywhere from one to ten dollars. Flimsy cages that look like they're made of coat hanger wire won't provide adequate support, so don't bother with these. Look for cages that are tall and made of heavy-gauge wire, with multiple, long anchor points that will extend securely into the soil. These may cost a few dollars more, but are worth the investment.

For determinate tomatoes, a 4- or 5-foot cage is usually sufficient. If you're using a cone-shaped cage, gardeners will want to add a stake to the plant as well. This will help keep the plant growing upright, and the cage will be less likely to tip over. Use a tall, heavy piece of wood or metal for the stake. Insert it into the soil about 2 inches away from the plant's stem, and secure it to the stem periodically as the plant grows.

Indeterminate tomatoes require heavy-duty support. They grow all season long and can produce plants from 6 to 10 feet tall, depending on the variety. That's a lot of foliage and a lot of weight, especially once fruit production starts. So plan accordingly. If a raised bed is situated near a wall, fence, or other vertical structure, gardeners can secure tomato cages to these for added support.

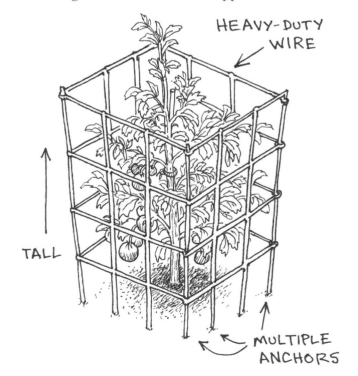

A good tomato cage offers significant support.

RECOGNIZING AND DEALING WITH PESTS AND PLANT DISEASES

Now is the time to start teaching your gardeners how to inspect for signs of pests or disease. They shouldn't encounter many, since the garden is new with fresh, healthy soil. If pests are found, it is no cause for alarm or a reflection on the gardener's ability. Help folks resist the urge to grab a can of bug spray.

There are many ways to organically manage pests and disease, including proper watering, providing air circulation to plants (by trellising and pruning), using protective barriers (such as floating row covers), eliminating habitats where pests and disease can proliferate, removing diseased material before it spreads, and crop rotation if you are gardening with a row method.

BENEFICIAL INSECTS AND HELPFUL PLANTS

The variety of crops grown in a community garden is a boon to diversity and helpful when attracting beneficial insects. Specific herbs and flowers growing alongside vegetable crops will discourage certain pests while also attracting beneficial insects. Collectively, your gardeners can decide to put in a plot, or multiple plots, designed to attract pollinators and beneficial insects.

GOOD BUGS–BAD BUGS

Insects will bring up insecurity with your gardeners; let them know that not all bugs are bad. (Similarly, if plants show signs of disease, don't let gardeners blame themselves; the problem is usually beyond anyone's control.) In fact, many bugs improve the health of the garden ecosystem. Pollinators such as bees and wasps help plants produce fruit, and ground-dwelling beetles and worms enrich the soil. Predatory insects control unwanted pests by feeding on them—for example, ladybugs and lacewings have a healthy appetite for aphids.

Simply put, a bug is bad if it's causing damage to the plant in any way that prevents gardeners from being able to grow the plant to maturity or to eat the fruit. In many cases, pest insects have short lifespans, or their damage is merely cosmetic. Remove them by hand and either squish them or drown them in a bucket of soapy water. Gardeners can also prune affected leaves and fruit and discard them. In the event of an infestation, spraying infested leaves with water will wash unwanted visitors away. As a last resort, use the least toxic chemical controls available, such as homemade soap spray, horticultural oils, or botanicals (but remember, these may kill the good bugs as well as the bad).

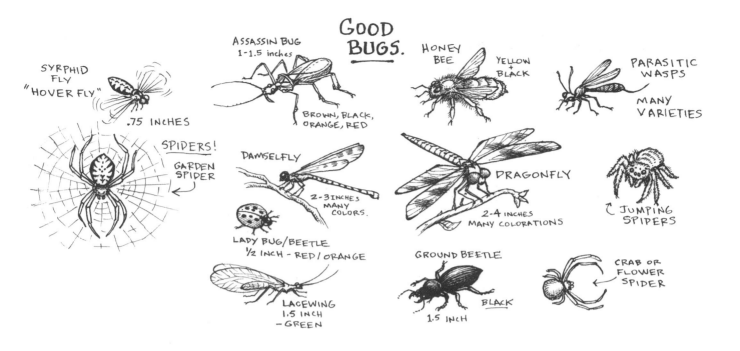

Plants that Attract Beneficial Insects

Plant	Attracts
Angelica	Lacewings, lady beetles, parasitic wasps
Anise	Lady beetles, parasitic wasps, tachinid flies
family *Asteraceae* (asters, daisies, sunflowers)	Bees, hoverflies, lacewings, lady beetles, parasitic wasps, tachinid flies
Dill	Bees, hoverflies, lady beetles, spiders, wasps
Lovage	Beneficial wasps, (shelters) ground beetles
Marigold	Hoverflies, parasitic wasps
Nasturtium	Spiders, ground beetles
Zinnia	Bees, lady beetles, parasitic wasps, parasitic flies

Bad Bugs

Bug	Description	Organic Antidote
Aphids	Aphids are small, sucking insects that eat the soft tissue in plants– particularly new growth. Look for them in the head of the plant or on the underside of leaves. They're about 1/10-inch long and green, black, brown, or gray in color. Aphids rarely cause severe damage to plants, but they do reproduce quickly, so eliminate them early if possible.	Wash off with a heavy stream of water or homemade soap spray (dissolve one tablespoon of dish soap into three cups of water).
Cabbage worms and loopers	A cabbage worm is the larva of a butterfly, and a cabbage looper is the larva of a moth. Both like to munch on the brassica family of plants (such as cabbage and broccoli), as well as leafy greens. Look for holes in leaves or leaves that have been reduced, at least in part, to their spines. The caterpillars have hearty appetites, so try to catch them while they're small. At full size, they're about an inch and a half long. The caterpillars can be difficult to see since they're green and blend in with the plants. Check the underside of leaves or in the head of the plant for piles of moist, dark green frass (poop).	Lure caterpillars off the plant with a stiff wire or stick. Then snip them with scissors or drop them into a pail of soapy water. Use a floating row cover to help prevent them from coming into contact with plants.
Cucumber beetle	Cucumber beetles primarily affect cucumbers, squash, and melons. There are two kinds—striped, which has a yellow body and three black stripes, and spotted, which is yellow with twelve black spots on its back. Both are about 1/4-inch long. Signs of infestation include chewed leaves and stems, and marks on fruit. The beetles also spread bacteria on plants when they munch on them, causing leaves to wilt.	Handpick and squish beetles, and prune off and destroy any plant parts that show signs of bacterial wilt. You can protect seedlings with a floating row cover.
Leaf miners	Leaf miners are larvae of small flies that live in and eat the inner membrane of plant leaves. You'll see the damage before you see the insect itself—look for dried brown patches or maze-like patterns on leaves.	Remove affected leaves, since it's hard to reach the insects inside the leaves. Floating row covers help prevent flies from laying their eggs in the first place.

Bug	Description	Organic Antidote
Slugs and snails	Slugs and snails eat all kinds of vegetation, including leaves, stems, and the fruit of plants. If you see large chunks missing from your plants, chances are a snail or slug is nearby. During the day they retreat to damp, shady spots. Look under big rocks, piles of grass clippings, or other debris-laden areas to find them. It's best to do this at dusk, at night with a flashlight, or on a rainy day.	Remove by hand, and eliminate their habitats as well (for example, your cabbage that's resting on the ground should be staked up). Repel them by putting a copper barrier around your bed (the flexible tape emits a natural electrical charge), or use non-toxic baits such as iron phosphate or beer (poured into a pie tin and sunk into the ground).
Squash vine borer	Squash vine borers prefer winter squash, zucchini and other summer squash, and, to a lesser degree, melon plants. The borers are larvae of moths that lay their eggs at the plant's base. Caterpillars develop and feed inside the stalk, migrating to the main stem. If you catch the larvae early, you can effectively control them. Check for dots of frass protruding from holes on the stem of the plant, near the base. If you see wilting vines or leaves, it may be too late to save the plant.	Use a knife to carefully cut the stem along its axis where you see signs of infestation. Split open the stem and look for the caterpillar—it will be cream colored and up to an inch long. Remove it with a toothpick or stiff wire, then squish it or snip it in half. Cover the hole in the stem immediately with moist soil. You can prevent egg laying by wrapping the lower stem of the plant in nylon stockings or aluminum foil, or by using a floating row cover (until the plant starts blooming, at which point it will need to stay uncovered so it can pollinate).
Tomato hornworm	Tomato hornworms are the larvae of hawk or sphinx moths and commonly affect tomatoes, as well as eggplants, peppers, and potatoes. The caterpillar is green in color with eight white V-shaped marks along its sides and a black hornlike protrusion from its rear end. At full size, it's three to four inches long. Even though hornworms are quite large, they blend well into plant foliage, so you'll probably notice damage to plants before you see the caterpillars themselves. Look for stripped leaves and piles of black frass on and around the plants.	Since they're so big, hornworms are easy to remove by hand. You can squish them, snip them with scissors, or toss them into a pail of soapy water. Or you could eat them! Some people even claim that the little ones taste like tomatoes!

HARVEST—OR NOT?

Don't be surprised if your first-time gardeners don't have a clue as to when to harvest their vegetables, or have perhaps lapsed in collecting their ripe produce.

When we see veggies in the grocery store, they often look quite different than in the garden, as outer leaves or other foliage has been removed. Some stuff is very recognizable—tomatoes and peppers, for instance—but some ripe vegetables, like Brussels sprouts or fennel, can cause confusion. In chapter 8, you'll find simple harvest techniques along with plant descriptions. Share this information with your gardeners through your communication channels, so they don't miss out on the peak of ripeness for their crops.

If your garden is a collective arrangement, set up a rotation of people to harvest produce.

In an allotment-style garden, where individuals grow the food for their own use, you can expect times in the garden when people don't harvest their produce. Try not to judge as you're looking at those beautiful crops going to waste—we all get busy and sometimes unforeseen circumstances disrupt the best intentions.

What can be done when there is an accumulation of unharvested produce? Whether yours is an allotment or collective garden, it is wise for the community to think through these possibilities at season's beginning, so all the gardeners know the rules related to unused food. Here are a few ways to manage harvest time.

Have a sharing signal

Many gardeners may know they can't tend their beds. By having a way to indicate that their bed is open for gleaning, they can save face with goodwill. One garden I know of has a "white rock" gleaning program. If a member is unable to harvest, they place white rocks (stored centrally) in their area for as long as they are unable to be there. This is a signal that others are free to harvest from the plot.

Have a notification system

If produce seems to be going to waste, give gardeners one week notice (through e-mail or other means) that produce will be picked and donated to a local nutrition program if they don't harvest it.

Of course, neither of these methods are required if gardeners talk to one another or know each other's habits. In the healthiest communities, sharing often happens naturally.

COMMON DISEASES

For the most part, diseases are rarely fatal to plants in small-scale production like a home or community garden (they can be devastating to industrial agriculture, however). But diseases can spread quickly, particularly in an environment where there are many beds in close proximity, so it's important to catch them early. Removal of affected plant parts is often enough to control the spread of infection.

Plant diseases are often contagious. Your gardeners need to know that when they're done working on, and disposing of, infected plants, they must make sure to wash hands and disinfect gardening tools to help prevent the spread of disease. If you are working in a situation where tools are being shared, this point cannot be over emphasized. If tools aren't disinfected and they are used by multiple gardeners, they will be disease carriers.

Here are a few common diseases that your gardeners might see in the summer growing season, along with their symptoms and methods for treating them.

Okay, enough about disease and pests! If your gardeners encounter problems that can't be identified or successfully treated, contact your county extension service. Trained horticultural experts can assist with garden problems, or enlist a Master Gardener who is especially knowledgeable in this area.

Common Diseases

Problem	Description	Organic Antidote
Blossom end rot	Blossom end rot can affect tomatoes, peppers, squash, and other fruiting vegetables but is most prevalent in tomatoes. It's caused by a calcium deficiency in the fruit and often occurs due to erratic weather as the fruit begins to set (if the plant gets too dry or too wet, its ability to absorb calcium from the soil is diminished). Blossom end rot is most often seen on the first fruit of the season as dark brown, leathery, sunken spots on the blossom (bottom) end of the fruit.	Pick and discard damaged fruit in the trash (and rest assured this isn't a life sentence for your plant— subsequent fruit probably will turn out just fine). Help prevent onset by watering attentively and trying to maintain a consistent moisture level in your soil—gardeners might try adding a layer of mulch. Watering deeply a couple of times a week is more effective than watering superficially every day.
Powdery mildew	Powdery mildew is a fungal disease that favors squash, cucumbers, and melon foliage. It's usually caused by conditions of high humidity, crowded plantings, or poor air circulation. You'll recognize it as powdery splotches of white or gray, most often on the top surfaces of leaves and stems of plants, and at times on lower leaf surfaces, flowers, buds, and fruit. Powdery mildew isn't fatal, but if enough of the plant is covered, it can become stressed and fruit quality can diminish.	Trim off any infected plant parts and discard them in the trash. Improve air circulation by thinning and pruning as appropriate, and make sure to water under foliage, not on top of it.

(continued on next page)

Problem	Description	Organic Antidote
Tomato blight	Many tomato diseases are lumped into the category of blight—early blight, late blight, and septoria leaf spot, to name a few. If your plant's leaves suddenly have brown curly edges, dark lesions, or bull's-eye splotches with concentric rings, take a photo of the infected foliage and compare it to images you find online or in a book. It's normal for leaves to dry out as a plant ages, so research is important to determine whether a plant is indeed infected. Blights are fungal diseases and can spread quickly to fruit and other plants. Sometimes blight can return the following season since the fungi live in the soil. Encourage your gardeners to be prompt and vigilant in treating infected plants. If only a few leaves are affected, there's a good chance the plant can be saved. But if most or all of the foliage is diseased, the plant's time is up and should be pulled and discarded in the trash (do not compost).	Remove affected plant parts and throw them in the trash. Gardeners can try applying a commercially available hydrogen peroxide solution to help kill the fungus, if it has only infected small areas of the plant. Overly wet conditions can encourage blight. Preventive techniques include proper watering and spacing plants to allow enough airflow between them. Trim leaves that are touching the ground to prevent soil backsplash from rain and watering. Gardeners might also add a layer of mulch around the base of the plant to help soil retain moisture.

THE NEED TO WEED

A less-than-exciting (but necessary) subject every garden must deal with is weeds. Most people hate weeding, yet it is a vital garden task. With intensive gardening, weeds are minimized because as the plants grow, they often crowd out weeds. Any weeds that do occur can easily be pulled. Row gardening is another story—weeds can become a major time suck.

Help your gardeners understand that weed management is critical in the community garden, because once weeds go to seed, they will create a much bigger problem the next season. Most garden weeds aren't dangerous or noxious, and pulling them requires less skill than diligence.

A popular question from beginning gardeners will be, "What do weeds look like?" An easy response is, if you didn't plant it, consider it a weed. In some instances, though, a weed can grow where an unfamiliar crop was planted, and gardeners can mistake the weeds for their vegetable plants. I've actually seen people trellising and pampering weeds, thinking they were a thriving crop (this situation usually causes great sadness when I break the news to them). Your local extension service will have online or other resources that can help gardeners identify weeds common to your area.

The other weedy issue is apathy, or in some cases, downright resistance. No matter how often you ask gardeners to weed around their plots or common areas, they don't want to do it. Or, you might get lucky and have a zealous weed puller in your community. If you're so gifted, make that person a crown (or halo) to wear around the garden, and hope their enthusiasm rubs off on the other gardeners!

FALL—WRAPPING UP AND CLOSING THE GARDEN FOR THE SEASON

You've learned by now that I'm writing from a northern perspective. Your garden may be able to grow year-round—that's awesome (and I'm jealous). But for those folks who have seasonal bookends for their gardens (and don't want to approach winter gardening just yet), autumn is the time when nature starts to wind things down. And, believe me, after the first season with your community garden, everyone will likely be ready for a break about then, anyway. The great thing about gardening is that enthusiasm always bursts forth again in the spring, so a little time off just helps rekindle energy for the next year . . . and the next year . . . and the next.

Based on where your garden is located, and your decisions about the annual life of your garden, you may be calling it quits (for the season!) when the weather starts to get cold in the autumn. And, of course, you'll want your gardeners to participate in cleaning up the garden in the fall, whether the community is organized as a collective or individual allotment garden.

Fall Education Topics

➡ Understanding Frost Tolerance Levels

➡ Garden Cleanup and Composting

➡ The First Garden Season: What Have We Learned?

The weeks just before and just after the average frost date are touch and go. It is called an *average* frost date for a reason—the exact date will vary from year to year. Many gardeners get anxious about their beloved tomatoes and other hot-season crops and want to milk every last drop of warmth out of the season, to get the most ripe fruit. A surprise frost can end those plans quickly, so encourage your gardeners to monitor the weather and plan accordingly. Many crops, however, can stand some cold temperatures. And some, like members of the cabbage family, taste even better after exposure to a few cold days. It is important for your gardeners to know what to harvest when, to avoid remorse on those first frosty days.

UNDERSTANDING FROST TOLERANCE LEVELS

Frost Tolerance of Vegetables

Sensitive (damaged by light frost)	Semi-Hardy (tolerates light frost)	Hardy (tolerates hard frost)
Basil	Arugula	Broccoli
Beans	Beets	Brussels sprouts
Cucumbers	Carrots	Cabbage
Eggplants	Cauliflower	Collards
Okra	Celery	Kale
Peppers	Lettuce	Kohlrabi
Summer squash	Peas	Onions
Tomatillos	Swiss chard	Parsley
Tomatoes		Radishes
Melons		Spinach
		Turnips
		Leeks

Light frost: 28 to 32 degrees F. Hard frost: below 28 degrees F.

GARDEN CLEANUP AND COMPOSTING

Many community gardens go dormant in the off-season. In the north, the off-season is fall and winter; in the south, it could be the super-hot days of summer, when nothing can grow due to extreme heat. Only you know when your garden community needs a rest. Some gardens go strong all winter long! (Specific approaches to year-round gardening are not included in the scope of this book, however.)

When it is time to wrap up the garden for the season, gardeners will need to know what's expected of them in terms of cleanup and prepping for next season. You'll have a list of communal tasks specific to your garden, such as collecting and storing all tools, winterizing water sources, and removing debris. Gardeners will need to know how they (individually) need to tidy up the garden areas they and their families have been tending.

When removing spent plants, avoid pulling them out by hand. Uprooting plants—especially ones with large root systems like tomatoes and squash—can be difficult and messy. But more importantly, turning the soil in this way is disruptive to your soil balance. All those tiny soil-dwelling organisms are doing a fine job of conditioning your soil and keeping it healthy, so disturb them as little as possible. Use pruning shears to cut off plants at the soil level; roots that remain should break down by next spring.

If your garden space (or available volunteer power) doesn't lend itself to a full-blown composting program, encourage your gardeners to engage in passive composting, which requires little effort other than setting the process in motion and letting nature go to work over the winter. Instead of throwing spent plant materials in the trash, gardeners can passively compost simply by cutting trimmings into small pieces and spreading them directly over their soil. The remains will start to decompose and immediately return nutrients to the soil. The trimmings will also act as mulch to help insulate the beds over the winter. If any pieces remain come spring, gardeners can remove them or gently mix them into the top layer of the soil.

Once the garden closes for the season it is a good time to encourage the gardeners to reflect on what worked in their individual gardens and what did not, and to take a few notes for next year. This is a good habit for new gardeners to get into (though, regretfully, most do not).

From a community perspective, now is also a good time to reconvene and let everyone discuss what did and didn't work in the garden. By listening to these experiences, the garden's education program and rules can be fine-tuned for the following season. Praise and complaints are the culmination of your program's first year—sharing these foundational experiences is essential to the garden's success in subsequent years. Take the time to hear it all, absorb the joys and the woes, and find a way to constructively channel that information back to the community. Your experiences will translate into valuable talking points and best practices for planning the community garden's second year.

The end—and the beginning

I'll bet you learned a lot your first year! Did you take on more than you could accomplish? Did everyone get tired mid-season and let things fall by the wayside? Did weeds drive you nuts? Did you figure out how to best communicate with your gardeners and get to know the particular personality of your group? Was the food you grew delicious? Did it help your gardeners or community? Was the space a haven for people of all types?

Your garden is now moving along with a life of its own. Each year you will find new challenges and solve old problems. New faces will add energy and original gardeners will return or move on. Ultimately, time will tell the story of your garden and how its existence will benefit your neighborhood and the people who live there.

The most important thing is that you did it! Good job. Rest up for a few months, absorb the lessons of your first year, and get ready to start again. Because, as the old adage says, "hope springs eternal," and, come the start of growing season, people will be anxious to be together and start growing. The best part? Now that your first year is over, it gets easier. Be proud. You've done something amazing that will be appreciated for years to come.

THE FIRST GARDEN SEASON: WHAT HAVE WE LEARNED?

 8. TWENTY-ONE VEGETABLES

To Sow, Harvest, Store, and Serve

ARUGULA
Eruca sativa

This fast-growing, spicy salad green, also known as salad rocket, is often ready for harvest at 4 weeks. Arugula seeds provide a continuous crop when planted every 2 to 3 weeks, except in the heat of summer, when the plants will bolt. Let a few plants go to seed and the arugula will come back on its own every year.

Start Plant seeds as soon as the soil is warm and where the plants will get plenty of sun. Plant early in the season and in cooler fall weather. Planting intensively, put one plant per square foot, or you can broadcast seeds over a square foot for baby greens.

Grow Add compost to soil that is kept loose and moist. Arugula also grows well in containers, with frequent watering.

Harvest To encourage continuous growth, gently pick the outer leaves, which are best when small and young.

Store and Serve Arugula keeps best when stored unwashed in a plastic bag. A paper towel placed in the bag will absorb extra moisture and keep leaves fresh.

Most commonly, arugula adds a spicy flavor to salads and sandwiches. Try making pesto with this versatile green, toss lightly sautéed arugula with pasta, or throw a handful into soups.

Don't judge each day by the harvest you reap but by the seeds that you plant.

—Robert Louis Stevenson

BEETS
Beta vulgaris

Beets are an easy-to-grow vegetable, with added value. Both the root and the greens are edible and full of vitamins. While red beets are most common, white, orange, and golden beets have a milder flavor and are great for roasting.

Start Before planting, work a 1-inch layer of compost into the soil. Sow beet seeds in full sun every 2 or 3 weeks, until the temperature reaches 75 degrees F. Sow again late in the season for a fall crop; beets like the cold. Plant seeds ½ inch deep and 2 inches apart. If you are planting intensively, you can plant 16 beets per square foot and harvest them small. For bigger beets, plant 9 per square foot.

Grow Seeds germinate within 10 days if kept moist. Continue to water regularly if the weather is dry, to prevent the beets from becoming woody.

Harvest When the greens are several inches tall, it is getting close to harvest time. Brush back soil to check size when the beet (a root crop) starts to protrude from the soil. Beets can be harvested at 1 inch, or up to 4 inches.

Store and Serve Separate the root from the beet greens, leaving 2 inches of the stem intact. Unwashed beets will keep in the refrigerator in a tightly closed plastic bag for up to 2 weeks. Greens stay fresh for a few days when wrapped in a damp paper towel and stored in the refrigerator in an open plastic bag, or when set in a jar of water in the refrigerator, and covered with a plastic bag.

Wash beet greens and cook like spinach or chard. Younger leaves are good in salads, as are grated beets. Scrub beets to remove dirt and peel older beets. Grilling, boiling and roasting all bring out the natural sweetness.

CABBAGE
Brassica oleracea

Cabbage is a cool-season crop with smooth or crinkly leaves. It can be harvested in the spring and fall. Related to other vitamin-rich brassicas like kale, broccoli, and Brussels sprouts, cabbage is often used in traditional ethnic foods such as sauerkraut and kimchee.

Start Cabbage is easy to grow from transplants or seeds. In a sunny spot, set out transplants in early spring, 1 to 2 feet apart, depending on size of head desired. Seeds will germinate best when the temperature is above 55 degrees F.

Grow Rich soil and plenty of fertilization and water will ensure vigorous growth. Mulch to keep weeds down and moisture in. In midsummer, sow a crop for fall harvest.

Harvest Cabbage heads are ready for harvest when they are tight and firm. Give the head a hard squeeze, and if the leaves feel loose, leave it for a while longer. Cut the stem below the head and don't pull the plant, as smaller heads often develop near the base. Cabbages that mature in cold weather grow very sweet.

Store and Serve Cabbage heads keep well in the refrigerator for several weeks, in a plastic bag. To keep longer, store upside down in a cool, dark place with good air circulation. Do not wash before storing, and remove outer leaves that wilt.

Peel away wilting leaves and wash the outside of the cabbage. Cut cabbage into quarters and remove the core with a knife. Shred it for coleslaw or cook by boiling, steaming, braising, or baking. Or use the leaves for stuffed cabbage. To avoid unpleasant odors, do not overcook. Use a stainless steel pot and cook until just tender. Place the leaves around a filling of meat or grain, and bake in the oven.

CARROTS
Daucus carota

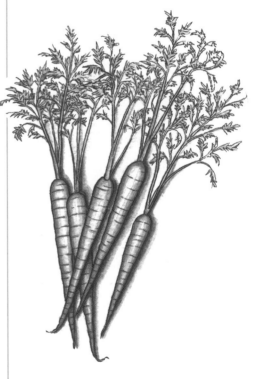

Homegrown carrots come in many colors and shapes and taste so much better than those from the supermarket.

Start Carrots grow best in sandy soil that is very loose and free of stones, so the carrots can easily push through. Sow seeds in the spring, 4 inches apart and in rows a foot apart. If planting intensively, plant 12 carrots per square foot.

Grow Weed diligently and mulch to retain moisture and speed germination. After a frost, cover carrot rows with a layer of shredded leaves or straw, and harvest them later in the fall.

Harvest Carrots are ready for harvest after about 2½ months of growing and when they are about ½ inch in diameter. The greens will be quite tall and it might be necessary to pull one out to see if the crop is big enough. Pull them out gently, or dig them out by hand or with a trowel.

Store and Serve Twist off the tops and store unwashed. Seal in airtight plastic bags and refrigerate. Do not put fresh carrots directly into the refrigerator, they will go limp. The greens are edible and can be kept in cold water. Freeze carrots by blanching them in boiling water for 5 minutes. Place them in ice water to stop the cooking, pack in a container, and store in the freezer.

Cooking enhances the natural sweetness of carrots—steam, boil, or bake. Scrub the dirt off gently and leave the outer layer on as it is a good source of vitamin A. Toss carrots in a bit of olive oil, then bake in the oven with other root vegetables. Raw carrots are well suited for juicing, or add peeled or grated carrots to a salad. The greens are also nutritious—throw them into a stock or chop them into salad.

CORN
Zea mays

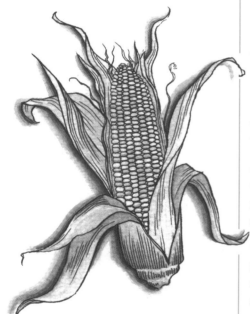

Corn has been domesticated in North America for 4,000 years. The taste of freshly picked sweet corn is unbeatable. Grow the kinds of corn that have a good track record for your climate, whether yellow, white, or multicolored .

Start Corn requires a lot of space in a vegetable garden and is susceptible to frost. Plant seeds only in well-warmed soil to guarantee germination. Add a lot of compost to the soil before planting, and sow in a sunny, wind-protected area.

Grow Plant seeds 1 inch deep with 3 feet between rows. If you are growing intensively, plant 1 seed per square foot. Keep weeds to a minimum to encourage strong growth in the first month. Roots are shallow and will spread out, so don't disturb them while weeding. Apply mulch to prevent weeds from coming back. In dry weather, water well.

Harvest When the ears have filled out, corn is ready to harvest. The silks dry up and the end of the ears feel rounded or blunt, rather than pointed. Pull back a bit of the husk to see if the kernels have filled out, and pierce a kernel to make sure the liquid is milky rather than watery.

Store and Serve Best eaten within a day or two of picking, corn loses its sweetness quickly. Refrigerate corn in the husk, spread out in a single layer. To freeze, blanch the cob in boiling water for 5 minutes, rinse under cold water. Freeze the cobs whole in a freezer bag, or remove the kernels for storing in a smaller container.

Just-picked raw young corn is best used in salads or salsas. Before using or cooking, shuck ears by peeling off the husk and removing the stringy threads, called corn silk. Cook corn for the shortest time possible. Five minutes for boiling, 10 minutes for steaming, and 15 minutes for oven roasting or grilling will keep the corn from toughening. Corn can also be grilled or roasted in the husks.

CUCUMBERS
Cucumis sativus

Cucumbers are a prolific, hot weather crop. Vining cucumber plants can be grown in any amount of space because they are climbers. Bush hybrids form a more compact plant. Varieties include slicing cukes that are oblongs with smooth dark green skin. Pickling cucumbers are smaller with bumpy rinds, and are crisp and firm. Asian cucumbers are long and slender, with fewer seeds.

Start Start cucumber plants indoors in peat pots, or direct sow in warmed soil. Plant 2 or 3 seeds an inch into the ground, spaced 12 inches apart (the same spacing goes for intensive gardening). Sprouting occurs in a few days in warm, moist soil. If the soil is heavy, mound it up before planting.

Grow Climbing cukes are planted around a trellis, wire netting, or other support. Growing vertically increases yield by improving air circulation, and makes good use of limited garden space. Bush or sprawling cucumbers do best when grown on a bed of straw or mulch.

Harvest Harvest when young, before the seeds are fully developed, for the most tender and tasty cukes. The ideal size is 6 to 8 inches for slicing cucumbers; 5 inches for pickling. Encourage fruit production by picking cucumbers as soon as they are ready.

Store and Serve Cucumbers do not store well because of their high water content. They will keep in the refrigerator for up to a week.

The best way to enjoy a surplus of cucumbers is to preserve them through pickling.

Enjoy cucumbers raw in salad either sliced or grated (no need to peel, the skins have nutritional value). Chilled cucumber soup is a refreshing summer treat.

EGGPLANT
Solanum melongena

This compact plant does best in climates with at least three months of warm weather. While most cultivars are purple, there are white, green, orange, and stripped eggplants. Various shapes of eggplant include round, long, and oval.

Start Getting eggplant off to a good start helps this finicky plant to produce an excellent harvest. Transplants benefit from not being planted too early. Wait until the soil has warmed, the days are sunny, and all threat of a cold night has passed, or growth will stall.

Grow Eggplant is a heavy feeder and grows well in rich, organic, well-drained soil, with an occasional blast of organic fertilizer. Space 12 inches apart (or 1 plant per square foot if growing intensively), and stake tall varieties. Mulch with light-colored straw to reflect the sun's heat. Water plants thoroughly during dry spells, being careful not to saturate leaves.

Harvest The fruits should be glossy at harvest, and the skin should bounce back when pressed with a finger. If the skin has become dull, the potential for bitterness is increased and the eggplant is overripe.

Store and Serve Eggplant is best eaten fresh, or kept on a counter at a cool temperature for up to a week. Store in the refrigerator only when necessary, and handle carefully, as bruising causes the eggplant to turn brown and bitter. Do not wash until ready to use.

Baked, stuffed, steamed, fried, roasted, grilled, or sautéed—there are so many ways to use eggplant in dips, stews, and casseroles. To prevent it from turning brown, prepare as closely to cooking time as possible. To cut down on oil absorption, let slices sit for ½ hour sprinkled with salt, wipe off with a paper towel, then cook. Peel only if the skin appears tough.

GARLIC
Allium sativum

Garlic is a rewarding crop that needs a long growing season. Planted in the fall, it will be one of the first crops to appear in the early spring. Garlic plants grow from garlic cloves, and it is best to plant varieties suited to your local growing conditions.

Start Midautumn, plant cloves in loose, fertile soil, pointed-end up. Space cloves 6 to 8 inches apart and push root side down about

3 inches deep. If you are planting intensively, you can plant 4 garlic cloves per square foot. Green shoots might come up but will die back with a freeze. Cover area with mulch.

Grow New shoots will emerge in the spring. Remove mulch. Some gardeners remove the top of the plant, called a scape, as it starts to curl, believing the energy will go into producing larger bulbs.

Harvest Depending on the amount of heat, garlic can be harvested midsummer or later, for bulbs that store well. Harvest when the lower leaves are turning yellow or brown, and the upper ones remain green. Use a digging fork to loosen soil, then gently lift area around the garlic head.

Store and Serve Set unwashed garlic heads in a row in an unheated pantry and out of the sun. Brush off the dirt and clip the roots after the outer skin becomes papery. Do not refrigerate. Unpeeled garlic can be put in a freezer bag and removed from the freezer as needed.

When peeling garlic, cut away any bruised spots and remove the bitter green sprout that sometimes emerges after garlic has been stored awhile. Chopping or crushing garlic cloves stimulates a process that brings out its health benefits. Add fresh, chopped garlic to tomato sauce, mashed potatoes, or chickpeas (when making hummus).

GREEN BEANS
Phaseolus vulgaris

Green beans are available in bush or pole varieties and many other colors. Both thrive even in poor soil and are ready for harvest in 7 or 8 weeks. Pole beans are good to grow in a small space as a climbing vine. The healthy bacteria in the roots of beans is a soil booster; it pulls nitrogen *into* the soil rather than leaching it out like other crops.

Start Don't plant beans too early, they are a summer crop. Green bean seeds will germinate only when the soil is warm and they are in full sun. Sow seeds every 2 to 3 weeks for a continuous yield.

Grow Decent garden soil amended with organic matter is all that is needed for good bean production. Do not add supplemental fertilizer, it is not necessary and will delay fruiting. For pole beans, set up a trellis or teepee of bamboo before planting. Bush beans do not need trellising. Plant seeds 1 inch deep and 2 inches apart. Water early in the day and avoid wetting the foliage.

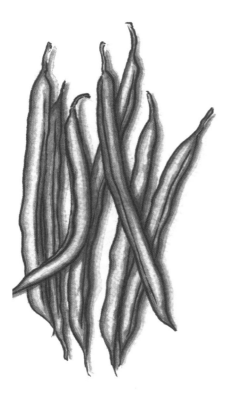

Harvest Pick beans at the immature stage, before the seeds inside have fully developed. Use scissors or snips to avoid tearing the plant. Check bean plants every other day and pick beans before pods mature, to ensure steady production.

Store and Serve Beans hold up best when stored in an air-tight container in the refrigerator. They will stay fresh for about 4 days. To keep longer, steam them for 2 minutes and freeze immediately. Beans are good for canning and pickling, two other methods for stretching an abundant crop.

The vitamins and minerals found in green beans are best retained when they are steamed for no more than 5 minutes.

KALE
Brassica oleracea var. *acephala*

Kale is a cold-hardy, resilient plant. The flavor differs depending on when it is harvested. Mild-tasting in spring, kale leaves may turn bitter in hot weather, while frost sweetens the taste of these antioxidant-rich greens. Multiple varieties are available, with various leaf shapes and colors.

Start Plant kale transplants in a sunny, well-drained spot early in the season. If sowing seeds, work compost into the soil and plant seeds ½ inch deep. Kale is a good crop to plant early in spring and late in the summer. Transplants or seeds grow best when planted a foot apart with 24 inches between rows or 4 per square foot for intensive spacing.

Grow Keep plants well watered; kale likes moist soil. Mulch under leaves to keep them from touching the ground and rotting. Pick off any withered leaves.

Harvest Harvest kale leaves before they are too old and tough. Start by cutting leaves from the outside when the plant is about 8 inches high. When the entire plant is cut 2 inches above the soil, the plant will sprout new leaves in about 2 weeks. Remove and discard any brown leaves.

Store and Serve Kale will keep for about a week, washed and wrapped in a damp paper towel and stored in the refrigerator in an open plastic bag. To freeze, wash and remove stems. Blanch in boiling water for 2 minutes. Rinse in cold water to stop cooking and store in freezer bags.

Remove stems by folding leaf in half and running a knife down the stem. Young, small leaves can be left intact and sliced into salads or thrown into a smoothie. Kale retains most of its volume when cooked, unlike spinach, and a pound yields 2 cups cooked. Sauté it, steam it, put it into soup, combine cooked kale with pasta, or make kale chips by tossing the leaves with oil and salt, then drying them out in the oven at the lowest setting.

OKRA
Abelmoschus esculentus

Okra is a traditional Southern vegetable that is also found in cuisines around the world. In the same plant family as hibiscus, the okra flower strongly resembles its cousin. Heirloom varieties can grow quite tall, with beautiful stems and colorful pods.

Start If planting okra from seeds, soak for 12 hours to soften the hard seed coat, and sow ½ inch deep. Early summer, once the soil is warm, is the best time to plant seeds or seedlings. Young plants can be grown in peat pots and planted directly in the soil so the roots are not disturbed.

Grow Okra can grow quite tall, up to 6 feet, and needs full sun, so plant where its shade will not block other plants. Water regularly during hot, dry spells. Remove pods that have grown too big.

Harvest Okra matures quickly and will be ready for harvest about 4 days after the plant flowers. Use scissors to cut the pods off when they are soft and no larger than 2 to 3 inches. Any bigger and the pod will be woody and inedible. Harvest every other day for continual production.

Store and Serve Do not wash okra. It does not store well—a few days at most in a perforated bag. Okra is best used fresh from the garden, or frozen or pickled at the height of freshness. To freeze, trim stems, blanch for 3 minutes in boiling water, and spread out on a tray. Once frozen, store in container.

Okra has a gummy substance that works as a thickener, but some find it slimy. Sauté, roast, and grill okra to eliminate slime, or dip in corn meal and deep fry. You can also wash just before use, pat dry, and cook with onions and tomatoes for a Southern favorite called gumbo.

ONIONS
Allium cepa

Onions come in a variety of shapes, colors, and flavors. They are easy to grow when varieties adapted to your specific climate are planted. A popular vegetable in cuisines throughout the world, onions store well and are thought to have many healthful properties.

Start It is best to grow onions from transplants or sets, as the seeds take a long time to germinate. Sets are small, dormant onions, and do better in cooler climates, while transplants are more successful in southern climates.

Grow Fertile, well-drained soil is best for growing all onions. Plant in early spring as soon as the ground can be worked. Keep the rows free of competing weeds, being careful not to damage the onions' shallow roots. Mulch to stifle weeds and hold in moisture. For sets, open a furrow 2 inches deep and place the sets pointed-end up about 6 inches apart. Fill in the furrow. If you are planting intensively, you can fit 4 onions per square foot.

Harvest For storage onions, harvest after the leaves have turned yellow. Use a rake to bend leaves over horizontally, diverting the energy to the bulbs. Let the bulbs emerge from the soil. When the tops turn brown, dig bulbs and leave them to dry in the sun. When the outer skins have dried, wipe off soil and remove tops, unless they will be braided.

Store and Serve Store in a cool, dry place or keep them in a mesh bag in a spot with good air circulation.

The versatile onion adds a tang to salads and sandwiches when raw and sliced thinly. Remove dry outer skins before using and cut the root last to avoid eye irritation. The longer onions are cooked, the sweeter they become. Caramelize onions by cooking them in a pan on low heat with butter or olive oil, stirring often until they are browned—a tasty base for soups and stews.

PEAS
Pisum sativum

There are peas that can be eaten pod and all (snow peas, sugar snaps), and those that must be taken out of the inedible pod before eating (shelling peas, commonly called English or garden peas).

Start Direct sow in late winter to early spring, spacing seeds 2 inches apart or 8 per square foot. Plant again 3 weeks later to extend the harvest, and again in midsummer for a fall crop. Use a legume inoculant on seeds prior to planting or in the planting hole to encourage healthy growth.

Grow In full or part sun, in moist, well-drained soil. Amend with compost prior to planting. Tall, climbing peas should be trellised, but shorter plants can trail.

Harvest Keeping your peas well picked encourages more growth and higher yield. For the best shell peas, pick plump, bright green pods. Shelling peas are sweet and succulent for about 3 to 4 days after being picked, and then start to become mealy and starchy. For tasty snap peas and snow peas, pick crisp smaller pods, which are generally sweeter and more tender than larger ones.

Store and Serve Keep fresh, unwashed peas in an open plastic bag in the refrigerator (to avoid sogginess) for no more than 2 to 3 days. Peas are high in sugar, which quickly turns to starch, reducing sweetness. Shell peas can also be taken out of the pod and dried and stored in an airtight container for use in soups.

All types of peas can be eaten raw in salads, steamed, stir-fried, or sautéed. You can also blanch them (boil in water for just a minute, then shock in ice cold water) and freeze for later use.

PEPPERS
Capsicum annuum

Peppers come in a variety of choices, from sweet to hot and from round and squat to long and pointy. Bell peppers are the most popular, though there is a pepper for every taste and cuisine, from sweet to fiery hot.

Start Peppers thrive on a long growing season with full sun and warm weather. They are sometimes a challenge to grow in cooler areas.

Grow Well-drained soil is essential, as standing water encourages root rot. Direct sowing of peppers from seed works best in very warm climates such as southern Florida. In cooler climates, seedlings are available at garden centers. Plant 12 inches apart, or 1 per square foot, with a layer of organic matter in each hole, to help retain moisture. Stake plants that are heavy with fruit.

Harvest Harvest sweet peppers gently with snips or a knife. Do not pull on the plant. Picking some peppers when green will encourage new growth. Depending on the variety, green bell peppers will become colored (red, orange, yellow, purple) when fully ripe—a surprise for new gardeners. If frost is forecast, pull up plants whole and hang upside down in a protected place; the fruits will continue to ripen. Hot chili peppers are best when left to ripen on the plant.

Store and Serve Peppers can be refrigerated for up to 5 days. Cored and diced peppers can be blanched and frozen, or pickled like cucumbers. Hot peppers can be air dried by stringing them together and hanging them in a dark area.

Peppers are best when eaten fresh from the garden. Chop for salads and salsa, or stuff with meat and rice and bake (clean out seeds first). Peppers are delicious when grilled, or roasted in the oven with other vegetables.

POTATOES
Solanum tuberosum

The potato is a starchy tuber from the nightshade family, and the uses, colors, and shapes of potatoes are infinite. Potatoes fall into three basic categories: baking, boiling, and all purpose.

Start Potatoes are grown from small tubers called seed potatoes. They prefer cool weather and should go into the ground in early spring. A small, whole potato or pieces of a potato with at least two eyes can be planted.

Grow In a sunny site, dig a trench 4 inches deep and spread organic compost in the trench. Plant seed potatoes a foot apart, with the eyeside up (or one plant per square foot if you are gardening intensively; plan for additional space when you begin to hill the potatoes). Cover with loose soil. When the plant is 6 inches tall, and every couple of weeks, mound the soil up (this is called "hilling"), in order to keep roots covered, support the plant, and keep the tubers from turning green and bitter. Keep soil moist in dry weather, being careful not to wet the foliage.

Harvest Flowering is an indication that the tubers are ready for harvest as "new" (small) potatoes. Once the vines die, dig up the potatoes or they may rot. Harvest on a dry day, gently, being careful not to puncture them. Use hands or a garden fork to work the soil and lift out the potatoes.

Store and Serve Separate blemished or cut potatoes and use them right away. Rub the dirt from the harvested potatoes; do not wash them. Store in paper or burlap sacks. Keep them in a cool place with good air circulation.

Use a brush to gently scrub the potatoes. Cut off green parts and any sprouts that have formed. Maximize health benefits by leaving the skins on. If peeled, the potatoes need to be cooked right away or they will turn brown. Use a fork to pierce cooking potatoes, when the fork goes in easily, they are done. Baked, boiled, grilled, fried, or sautéed, potatoes are delicious cooked many ways, and when added to stews and soups.

RADISHES
Raphanus sativus

Radishes are one of the fastest growing garden vegetables and come in a variety of shapes and levels of spiciness. Because they are fast growers, radishes are a good crop for children.

Start Direct sow seeds ½ inch deep and 2 inches apart in spring and fall. If you are planting intensively, you can plant 16 radishes per square foot. Plant seeds in full sun. Radish seeds can be planted every two weeks for multiple crops per season, except during the hottest months. If planting in rows, when the plants are a week old, thin to an inch apart for best results.

Grow Common salad radishes are a rapidly growing, cool-climate root vegetable. Cold-hardy autumn and winter radishes can be harvested over a long period. Plant seeds in rich soil and use mulch to protect plants.

Harvest Radishes are ready approximately 3 weeks after planting. Harvest as soon as radishes are mature. Do not leave in the ground too long or they will become woody and cracked.

Store and Serve Remove the radish tops, wash the radishes and store in an opened plastic bag in the refrigerator. Don't toss radish greens, wash the greens and store separately.

Radishes are vitamin-rich and can be used sliced in salads, stir-fries, stews, and soups. Radishes dipped in butter and salt are a delicious snack. Grate radishes into coleslaw or egg and potato salads. Add the greens to salads, use as a lettuce substitute on a sandwich, or cook in a stir-fry or stew.

SPINACH
Spinacia oleracea

Spinach is a fast-growing, cold-weather vegetable that yields profusely in the spring and fall. Plants will bolt (go to seed) in hot weather and become inedible.

Start   Plant in rows early in the spring, even in barely thawed ground, and in late summer. Sow seeds ½ inch deep and 2 inches apart, in rows spread 8 inches apart. If you are planting intensively and plan to harvest baby leaves frequently, plant 16 seeds per square foot.

Grow   Spinach will grow well in both full sun and in partial shade. Roots are shallow, so keep weeds down and soil moist with mulch. Plant successively in early spring and late summer for a continuous supply.

Harvest   Spinach is ready when there are 5 to 6 leaves on the plant. Snip off outer leaves about an inch away from the stem, letting the inner leaves mature. Spinach plants keep producing as long as the weather is cool. Harvest leaves before they are too mature and turn bitter.

Store and Serve   Spinach will keep in the refrigerator for up to one week. Wash leaves and pat dry thoroughly, to prevent spoilage. Wrap in a paper towel and place in an open plastic bag. If leaves wilt, revive in a bowl of ice water for a few minutes. To freeze, blanch leaves in boiling water for a minute, run under cold water, drain, and store in airtight container.

Mature leaves may have fibrous stems that need to be removed before using. Fresh spinach makes a healthy, dark green salad, or can be substituted for basil when making pesto. Spinach reduces greatly when sautéed or steamed: 3 pounds of raw leaves reduces to 2 cups. Bake spinach in a quiche or lasagna.

SUMMER SQUASH
Cucurbita pepo

Summer squash is a warm-season vegetable with a diversity of shapes, colors, and sizes. The most popular varieties are the cylindrical-shaped zucchini in green and yellow, the scallop or patty pan that is round and flattened, and the crooknecks.

Start   Plant seeds 1 inch deep in good sun when the danger of frost has passed, in early or midsummer. For a fall harvest, plant again in late summer. For row gardening, sow 2 to 3 seeds 36 inches apart. With intensive gardening, plant 1 seed per square foot and, in a raised bed, consider planting on the edge, so plants can sprawl out and not take up limited bed space. A few plants will yield many squash.

Grow Working compost into the soil where summer squash will grow improves drainage—important to the crop's success. Only the female squash sets fruit, and is identified by a tiny squash below the blossom. Early flowers are males and can be harvested for stuffed squash blossoms.

Harvest Summer squash can be harvested as baby squash, or when individual fruits reach 6 to 8 inches. Zucchinis are best when the skins are glossy. Avoid letting squash get overripe and too large. Squash grow fast, so pick every day or two for a continuous harvest.

Store and Serve Generally squash does not store well. Young squash are immature and bruise easily, so handle with care. To keep squash up to two weeks, preserve freshness by placing the unwashed vegetables in a plastic bag, squeezing out the air, and wrapping tightly. Store in the crisper section of the refrigerator.

Summer squash is very versatile and can be sliced, brushed with oil and cooked on the grill, roasted in the oven, or steamed. Summer squash has many uses in baking as well.

SWISS CHARD
Beta vulgaris subsp. *cicla*

This relative of the beet is favored for its often brightly colored leaves and stems, as well as its long growing season. One of the healthiest vegetables, it is full of vitamins and minerals. Versatile chard also has a place among ornamentals. Perpetual chard bears leaves over a long season, with new leaves emerging after picking.

Start Plant seeds approximately ½ inch deep and 12 inches apart, early in the season. If you are planting intensively, you can plant 2 to 4 plants per square foot (depending on how frequently you plan to harvest.)

Grow Water weekly and spread mulch to conserve moisture. Swiss chard also does well in seaside gardens, as it tolerates salt-laden winds. Chard grows well in cool weather or heat, and will only stop producing after a hard freeze.

Harvest Trimming the leaves improves flavor. They can be cut from the plant when they are about 3 inches long, or not more than 10 inches. Cut full-size leaves from the outside, and the plant will produce all season.

Store and Serve Swiss chard is best stored unwashed, to discourage spoilage. Squeeze as much air out of the storage bag as possible. Excess chard can be blanched and then frozen, to add to soups later.

Chard tastes best in the early spring and fall. Chop up the leaves and prepare like spinach, removing the midrib first. The midrib can be chopped and used like celery in cooking. Soups, casseroles, salads, and pasta are all enhanced by the addition of cooked-down chard.

TOMATILLOS AND GROUND CHERRIES
Physalis sp.

Tomatillos and ground cherries belong to the nightshade family. Both grow in an inedible paper-like husk, though their tastes are different. Tomatillo fruit is about the size of a walnut, and has a tart flavor. Ground cherries are bite-sized snacks with a sweeter flavor. Tomatillos grow upright up to 4 feet tall, while ground cherries sprawl.

Start Tomatillos and ground cherries need a long growing season with plenty of sun and heat. Start with seedlings purchased from a nursery.

Grow Set plants 2 to 3 feet apart in well-drained, warm soil. The plants are self-infertile and must have another plant close by to pollinate. If you are gardening intensively, plant ground cherries on a corner or edge of a raised bed so they can sprawl. Tomatillos take up a lot of room so account for 2 to 4 square feet for the mature plant. Also, tomatillos are very prolific so you might share one plant with several friends and free up space for more crops that way.

Harvest Pick tomatillos while they are deep green and the husk has changed from green to tan, or when the fruit busts through the husk. Left to ripen on the vine, they will turn yellow or purple with a bland taste. Ground cherries ripen from green to yellow-gold.

Store and Serve Tomatillos will keep for months in a cool spot with good ventilation. Spread them out in one layer without removing the husks, and do not store in a plastic bag or they will spoil. Canning is another way to preserve tomatillos.

Tomatillos are a tart-tasting staple of Mexican cooking, used in salads, tacos, and sandwiches. Ground cherries are used raw as a dessert, though they are more commonly used for jam, baked into pies, or cooked for a sauce on cakes and puddings.

TOMATOES
Lycopersicon esculentum

Due to their mass popularity, tomatoes are considered the king of garden vegetables. Tomato shapes include oblong, ruffled, plum, bite-sized cherries, and fruit that can weigh up to a pound. Tomatoes come in many colors: red, white, yellow, orange, green, purple, and striped.

Start Tomatoes need a long, warm growing season with full sun. They are best started in the garden as transplants.

Grow For optimal instructions, see page 149. You can also dig a hole twice the size of the root ball and put in a handful of compost. Plant up to the top set of leaves. Be ready with stakes or cages to support the fast-growing plants and keep them off the ground. Pinch off side shoots of indeterminate plants. You will place one plant per square foot if you are gardening intensively and plan on pruning and supporting your tomatoes. If you are going to let them go wild, leave more space.

Harvest Promptly harvest ripe fruit to relieve stress on the plants. Ripe tomatoes are deep in color and firm to the touch. Large beefsteak and plum varieties are good for sauce. Both ripen later than other varieties.

Store and Serve Store tomatoes indoors, on a counter, at room temperature —do not refrigerate, as this causes the flavor to break down. Large crops can be frozen, canned, or dried. For easy keeping for winter use, blanch tomatoes in boiling water, slip off the skins, and store in a freezer bag.

Straight-from-the-garden tomatoes are tasty in sandwiches (try them on a BLT), salsa, or sauce for pasta. Use frozen tomatoes in winter soups and stews.

RESOURCES AND BOOKS

RESOURCES

American Community Gardening Association

The ACGA is a binational organization supporting sustainable community gardens in the United States and Canada. This member-driven organization has been providing leadership, networking, and advocacy since 1979. Their website, www.communitygarden.org, is a wealth of information on many of the topics covered in this book, and others, including funding sources, templates, regional resources, training, events, and more.

In addition, ACGA facilitates a weekend workshop called "Growing Communities," which is offered all over the United States and Canada yearly by various groups (maybe like yours) who want to start their community gardens out on the right foot or evolve more positively. Contact the ACGA for more info on this powerful program.

Asset Based Community Development

Asset Based Community Development is a popular, common-sense approach to community organizing that was first articulated in the 1990s. ABCD's positive method focuses on what assets groups have, rather than what they don't have, and utilizes those resources to create outcomes that reflect their community. This methodology works through group processes and connects individuals, neighborhoods, and partner organizations in a positive, proactive way. A good book to read on this is *Building Communities from the Inside Out: A Path Toward Finding and Mobilizing a Community's Assets* (Center for Urban Affairs and Policy Research, 1993). Websites include ABCD Institute: www.abcdinstitute.org, and ABCD In Action: abcdinaction.ning.com.

Extension Services

In the United States, the extension service in each state is a wealth of relevant gardening information for your specific growing area. Many extension service websites offer information on pest identification, disease control, seasonal gardening guides, and more. Do some research and connect with your local extension—the resources will be invaluable. You'll find a list of all land grant universities (extension services) in the United States at http://www.csrees.usda.gov/qlinks/partners/state_partners.html.

Cornell University is like the mother ship for extension services. Founded in 1865, Cornell is one of the original land grant colleges formed to teach practical agriculture, among other topics. Their agriculture department is robust and provides numerous research-based, online resources regarding soil contamination, pest and disease control, and more. Here are three examples that I like:

Pest and disease information:
http://www.nysipm.cornell.edu/factsheets/vegetables/default.asp

Soil in relation to community gardens:
http://cwmi.css.cornell.edu/healthysoils.htm

Vegetable diseases:
http://vegetablemdonline.ppath.cornell.edu

In addition to online resources, local extension services have Master Gardener programs. Training varies from state to state but generally, Master Gardeners must take exam-based training, serve for a given period of time as an intern (for example, in Illinois it is one year plus 60 hours of public-facing volunteer time). After the internship period, the title Master Gardener may be used. Annually, Master Gardeners must do a set number of public-facing volunteer hours to maintain their status, while helping the general public by answering questions on a variety of gardening topics. Master Gardeners and community gardens are a great fit! They need hours—you need help! Find your local Master Gardener coordinator and make friends. You'll be glad you did.

Community Organizing
Citizen's Handbook:
http://www.citizenshandbook.org/1_00_intro_organizing.html

Center for Community Change:
http://comm-org.wisc.edu/papers97/beckwith.htm

On the Commons:
http://onthecommons.org/work/commons-network

Garden Planning and Design
Community Garden Design:
http://www.charretteinstitute.org/charrette.html
Raised-Bed Planning: www.gardeners.com.
This website is my favorite. Not only is the drag-and-drop interface incredibly easy to use, but it utilizes the intensive gardening method

described in this book. In addition to providing a visual grid for a raised bed, it automatically provides growing information for the plants selected in the grid. A great tool. I have used it for years to teach countless gardeners.

Gardens and Communities

Rutgers University Study on Community Gardens, 2012:
http://communitygarden.rutgers.edu/files/Lawson%20and%20Drake%20community%20garden%20survey%20report.pdf

Beginning Urban Farmers:
http://www.beginningfarmers.org/urban-farming/

Holidays: Community Garden Food Celebrations

www.holidayinsights.com/moreholidays.
In the United States, there are lots of holidays that are a bit wacky (and no doubt sponsored by corporations) that are fun to note (like National Cookie Day on December 4). Some of these holidays are vegetable- or food-related (National Picnic Day in April or National Celery Day in March), and you might be able to tie one in with a garden event. For our friends in Canada and abroad, you are more reserved (and dare I say, classy) with your holidays, but, regardless, this site lists the good, the bad, and the wacky around the world. Have some fun!

The Nonprofit Business of Gardening

Nonprofit Guidelines:
http://www.irs.gov/Charities-&-Non-Profits

Nonprofit Governance:
http://www.irs.gov/pub/irs-tege/governance_practices.pdf

Juno Consulting: http://junoconsulting.net

Axelson Center for Nonprofit Management:
http://www.northpark.edu/axelson

Council of Nonprofits: www.councilofnonprofits.org

OMRI—Organic Materials Review Institute

www.omri.org

Organizing Your Volunteers

www.volunteerspot.com

www.doodle.com

Seed Sources

Baker Creek Heirloom Seeds: www.rareseeds.com

Bounty Beyond Belief: www.bbbseed.com

Botanical Interests: www.botanicalinterests.com

Renee's Garden: www.reneesgarden.com

Seed Savers Exchange: www.seedsavers.org

Territorial Seeds: www.territorialseed.com

Home Garden Seed Association: www.ezfromseed.org

Security

www.padlockoutlet.com/1175LH-Master-Lock-Pro-Series-Resettable-Combination-Lock.html

Soil Calculator

www.gardeners.com/Soil-Calculator/7558,default,pg.html

BOOKS

Bartholomew, *Mel. 2005. All-New Square Foot* Gardening. Brentwood, Tennessee: Cool Springs Press.

Bucklin-Sporer, Arden, and Rachel Kathleen Pringle. 2010. *How to Grow a School Garden.* Portland, Oregon: Timber Press.

Colvin, Gregory L. 2006. Fiscal Sponsorship: 6 Ways to Do It Right. San Francisco: Study Center Press.

Connors, Tracy Daniel. 2011. *The Volunteer Management Handbook.* Hoboken, New Jersey: Wiley.

Deardorff, David, and Kathryn Wadsworth. 2011. *What's Wrong With My Vegetable Garden?* Portland, Oregon: Timber Press.

Editors of *Cooking Light* magazine, and Mary Beth Burner Shaddix. 2013. *Pick Fresh Cookbook: Creating Irresistible Dishes from the Best Seasonal Produce.* Birmingham, Alabama: Oxmoor House.

Forkner, Lorene Edwards. 2013. *The Timber Press Guide to Vegetable Gardening in the Pacific Northwest.* Portland, Oregon: Timber Press.

Hart, Rhonda Massingham. 2011. *Vertical Vegetables and Fruit: Creative Gardening Techniques for Growing Up in Small Spaces.* North Adams, Massachusetts: Storey Publishing.

Iannotti, Marie. 2013. *The Timber Press Guide to Vegetable Gardening in the Northeast.* Portland, Oregon: Timber Press.

Kretzmann, John P., and John L. McKnight. 1993. *Building Communities from the Inside Out: A Path Toward Finding and Mobilizing a Community's Asset. Evanston, Illinois*: The Asset-Based Community Development Institute.

Krevelen, Jean Ann Van. 2010. *Grocery Gardening: Planting, Preparing, and Preserving Fresh Food.* Brentwood, Tennessee: Cool Springs Press.

Newcomer, Mary Ann. 2013. *The Timber Press Guide to Vegetable Gardening in the Mountain States.* Portland, Oregon: Timber Press.

Taylor, Lisa, and the Gardeners of Seattle Tilth. 2011. *Your Farm in the City: An Urban-Dweller's Guide to Growing Food and Raising Animals.* New York: Black Dog & Leventhal.

Wallace, Ira. 2013. *The Timber Press Guide to Vegetable Gardening in the Southeast.* Portland, Oregon: Timber Press.

Walliser, Jessica. 2013 *Attracting Beneficial Bugs to Your Garden.* Portland, Oregon: Timber Press.

METRIC CONVERSIONS

inches	centimeters
1/10	0.3
1/6	0.4
1/4	0.6
1/3	0.8
1/2	1.3
1	2.5
2	5.1
3	7.6
4	10
5	13
6	15
7	18
8	20
9	23
10	25
20	51
30	76

feet	meters
1	0.3
2	0.6
3	0.9
4	1.2
5	1.5
6	1.8
7	2.1
8	2.4
9	2.7
10	3
100	30
1,000	300
10,000	3,000

1 cup .... 16 tablespoons .... 250 milliliters
1 pound ...... 16 ounces .... 454 grams

Temperatures
$°C = \frac{5}{9} \times (°F - 32)$
$°F = (\frac{9}{5} \times °C) + 32$

ACKNOWLEDGMENTS

During my sad days as a corporate wonk, I traveled a lot—up to 80 percent of the time—and I devoured books at a ravenous pace. I usually looked forward to reading the acknowledgments. Particularly when I had really enjoyed a book, the acknowledgements were like the last precious crumbs of a delicious meal.

Some were perfunctory and to the point—lists of names, sometimes with a morsel of explanation. Some were like those train wreck Academy Awards speeches, but instead of waiting for the orchestra to overpower the weeping pontificator, I could just turn the page and hope for a book club guide or something to get the final, sensible, echo of the author's voice.

While reading these acknowledgments, I always wondered what I would say if (and now when) I ever wrote a book. I guess this is it.

I love Timber Press. Growing up in Oregon, and always being a garden geek, I admired and idolized them for years. Being allowed into the inner sanctum was a privilege and thrill I will never forget. Nor will I forget the excellent guidance, patience, and new author therapy sessions provided by my acquiring editor Mollie Firestone and project editor Julie Talbot. I am grateful to Patrice Silverstein, who helped turn a manuscript into this book, to Andrew Beckman, for his attention when I was in town for meetings (and patience with my newbie questions), and to all the other lovely, smiling, helpful people who make a book like this happen. They have a place in my heart forever.

Much like a community garden, I learned in the process of this book that I am a collaborator vs. a lone author. And without the lovely and talented Zazel Loven—who helped with the case studies, plant descriptions, general editing, and frequent pep talks—well, I don't know what I would have done. Teresa Gale contributed with the work in chapter 7, and her attention to detail and sense of humor leave me in awe and delight, in equal measure. Lindsay Shepherd also assisted with the plant descriptions and chimed in on the volunteer section—her specialty; Alexandra Nelson shared her decades of wisdom on fundraising and nonprofit juju. The words they added helped a lot, but their support and candor meant everything.

My friend Lisette let me camp out in her upstairs loft to write (but only if I promised not to give her dog, Remy, too many cookies during the day). Without the solitude (and dog kisses), this book wouldn't have happened.

My beloved husband, Peter Wigren, listened to it all, ad nauseam, and his comment was always a truly enthusiastic, "I can't wait to read it!" He's done a great job of putting up with my particular brand of crazy for the past umpteen years and for that, and a million other reasons, I adore him. He is also a kick-ass gardener.

(Is the orchestra starting to play? I'm almost done.)

Finally. . . I want to thank my parents for living through the Great Depression, World War II, and the rest of the decades of our twentieth-century great American story, and for sharing their adventures, strength, and advice. Their World War II valor on the battlefield (my father was in the Allied occupation forces) and on the home front (my mother was a Rosie the Riveter) imparted to them a strength that they did everything in their power to make sure I inherited (whether I wanted to inherit it or not). Their "you can do it" attitude inspired Peterson Garden Project, this book, and, frankly, every other good thing that has come my way in life.

I especially credit my father, Kenneth Minikel, for instilling in me a passion for growing food and setting an excellent example of the power of active community participation. I would like to honor his life as an extraordinary, ordinary guy by dedicating this book to his beloved memory.

Kisses to you, gardening friends. Do your best out there. Thanks for reading this book.

Kenneth Minikel
1927–2013

INDEX

501c3 status, 61, 85–87, 91, 93

A

ABCD (Asset Based Community Development) approach, 18–19, 40
access to gardens
  for fresh food, 28, 36, 52, 60, 72
  giving information to volunteers for, 106, 107
  locating for convenient, 31, 32, 37
  removing obstacles to, 60
  security, 72–73
  See also fences
accessibility
  Americans with Disabilities Act (ADA) compliance, 76
  as design factor, 80
  of raised beds, 83
accounting professionals, 97, 111
ACGA (American Community Gardening Association), 94, 96
acorn squash, 144
ADA (Americans with Disabilities Act) compliance, 76
aesthetics of gardens, 60, 75
affordable housing groups, 54
agendas
  first community meeting, 40–41
  second community meeting, 46
  third community meeting, 77, 79
  people with other, 42
  template for, 38–39
agreements
  for checking account management, 98
  hold harmless waivers, 96, 105, 107, 108, 111, 112
  media permissions, 96–97, 105
  MOU (Memorandum of Understanding), 87–89
  with private land owners, 61–62
  short-term land, 61, 75
  signing by board members, 90
allotment gardens
  accommodating light needs in, 76
  description, 66–67
  fencing, 72
  harvesting in, 112, 160
  plant supports in, 155
  position of water source, 64
American Community Gardening Association (ACGA), 94, 96
AmeriCorps, 30
aphids, 156, 158
A-P-I (Assume Positive Intentions), 49–50
appreciation, expressing. *See* expressing appreciation
artists, 54, 119
arugula (*Eruca sativa*), 148, 169
asparagus, 137
Asset Based Community Development (ABCD) approach, 18–19, 40
Asteraceae, 157
attorneys, 88, 94, 111
Attributes of a Successful Group list, 40, 44, 77
autumn. *See* fall

B

banks
  as funding sources, 98
  as partners, 54
basil, 148
beans. *See* green beans
beds. *See* inground beds; raised beds
beehives, 72
beets (*Beta vulgaris*), 148, 170
bell peppers. *See* peppers
benches, 71, 72
berry patches, 67
Biernot, Atsuko, 27
bike racking of topics, 42, 43, 48
biodiversity, 141
black gold. *See* compost and composting
blights, 162
blossom end rot, 161
blueberries, 137
boards and board members, 87, 88–90
bolting, 68, 169, 182
brassica family, 158
Breadsmith, 26
broadcast sowing, 147

broccoli, 148
Brownie troops, 28
BrownPaperTickets, 104, 105
budgets and budget needs, 91, 97–98
bugs. *See* insects
build / building
  days, 108
  educational mandate as influence on, 75
  fall as good time for, 109
  and mission objectives, 75
  See also individual case studies, 21-33
bush beans. *See* green beans
Business and Professional People for the Public
  Interest, 87
business concerns
  501c3 status, 61, 85–87, 91, 93
  boards and board members, 87, 88–90
  bylaws, 90
  money management, 97–99, 111
  resources for assistance with, 87
  sales tax, 92
  volunteers with business skills, 110–111
  See also agreements; fundraising; insurance; liability
businesses, local
  donations from, 21, 23, 25, 27, 93
  as sources of land, 61
  as sources of volunteers, 103
  as sponsors of workdays, 110
butternut squash, 144
bylaws, 90

C

cabbage (*Brassica oleracea*), 148, 170–171
cabbage family, 158, 165
cabbage worms and loopers, 158
cages, 155, 185
Canada, hardiness data, 132
carrots (*Daucus carota*), 148, 171–172
case studies, 21–33
caterpillars. *See* cabbage worms and loopers; squash
  vine borer; tomato hornworm
cauliflower, 148
Certified Organic label, 143
charrette process, 77–79
checking accounts, 98
chemicals
  in fertilizers, 140, 141
  and general water supply, 65
  recycled materials free of, 82
  in soil, 62
  in treated lumber, 82

Chicago (IL)
  park district mandate, 63
  weather, 109
  World War II victory gardens in, 129
  See also Peterson Garden Project
children
  elementary school gardens, 29–30
  involved in gardening tasks, 26, 28
  play area as garden amenity, 72
  radishes as a good crop for, 181
  watering jobs for, 152
chives, 148
churches. *See* religious organizations
Citizens Committee on the Homeless (Santa Cruz,
  CA), 31
cleanup, 120, 125, 166
climbing plants, 154. *See also* cucumbers; green beans;
  peas
clubs as partners, 54
collaborative process. *See* charrette process
combo gardens, 67
common areas
  for dogs, 107
  maintenance chores in, 106, 109, 112, 160, 163
communication methods
  about regularly scheduled workdays, 110
  age-appropriate, 50–51
  channels for reporting safety concerns, 96
  designated stations at gardens, 80–81, 130
  for diverse populations, 36, 51, 97
  encouraging gardeners in, 107
  informational flyers, 42
  for organizing a meeting, 37
  with outside volunteer groups, 113
  overcommunication, 50–51
  social media, 42, 50, 92, 107, 130
  using graphic designers and marketing
    professionals, 111
community food gardens
  benefits of, 10, 117
  case studies, 21–33
  defined, 11–12
  support systems for, 59, 60
Community Homes Garden (Fargo, ND), 25
community organizing, 17–18
Community Supported Agriculture (CSA), 29, 31
compost and composting, 68–70, 140–141, 166
consensus
  in garden design, 77–79, 81, 156
  on garden type, 67
  harnessing the power of, 18

consensus (*continued*)
   importance of, 48, 61
   resolving conflicts, 48
   on short-term gardens, 61
   See also mission and mission statements
cooking and serving vegetables. *See individual plant profiles*, 169-185
cooking areas in gardens, 72
cooking educational programs, 30, 52, 117–118
cool season crops, 145
corn (*Zea mays*), 148, 172–173
corporate world mentality, 49–50
costs, researching, 73, 81. *See also* budgets and budget needs
cress, 148
crime deterrence, 20, 60, 107
crop diversity, 140–141, 156
crops
   cool and hot season, 145
   labeling, 146
   life cycle for direct-seeded, 148
   for part-and dappled sun, 134
   soil-boosting, 175
   space-hogging, 135, 144
   value/space comparisons, 135
crowd-sourced funding platforms, 92
CSA (Community Supported Agriculture), 31
cucumber beetle, 158
cucumbers (*Cucumis sativus*), 148, 154, 172–173

D

deer, 73
design process, 76–81
development plans, 91
disabilities, people with, 54
diversity and diverse populations
   celebration of, 24
   communication methods for, 36, 51, 97
   community gardens as supportive of, 36
   See also Growing Together Community Gardens; The Homeless Garden Project; Sahara Seniors Garden

documentation
   importance of media permissions form, 96
   operating budget as, 98
   of special events, 121, 123
   of workdays, 110, 113
dogs in the garden, 107
donors. *See* funding sources
Donors Forum, 87

dream gardens. *See* visioning exercises
driving forces in garden genesis
   celebrating cultural heritage, 24
   combining environmental work and hands-on project, 30
   creating social change peacefully, 30
   fellowship, 26
   recruiting a new generation of gardeners, 22
   reducing homelessness, 33
   role in mission development, 20
   social and economic justice ideals, 28

E

Ecosource (Mississauga, Ontario, Canada), 23
educational programs
   for children, 26
   collaborating with support organizations, 52, 60
   on compost and composting, 68–70
   cooking, 30, 52, 117–118
   importance of basic instruction, 132
   Montessori doctrine and hands-on learning, 29
   new gardener workshops, 139
   in satellite school gardens, 28
   suggested themes by season, 133, 139, 153, 164
educational resources
   books and Internet research, 129
   extension services, 62, 68, 131, 161, 163
   friends, neighbors, family members, 129
   See also educational programs; Master Gardeners/ expert gardeners
eggplant (*Solanum melongena*), 148, 159, 174
Egnal, Martha, 29, 30
employee gardens, 11, 61
empty lots, 61
endive, 148
English peas. *See* peas
enthusiasm cycles, 109–110, 114, 164
equipment and tools
   for accessing water, 64
   basic supplies, listed, 71
   one-time/occasional use of, 71
   use policies, 107
Europe, hardiness data, 132
EventBrite, 104, 105
events
   activity ideas by month, 126–127
   fundraising, 29, 91–92
   potluck, 125
   social, 119–120
   stages for, 72, 81, 120
   using event professionals, 111

volunteer appreciation, 121
Executive Service Corps, 87
expert gardeners. *See* Master Gardeners/expert
    gardeners
expressing appreciation
    as agenda item, 39, 41, 79
    as key element in management program, 103, 113
    at orientation, 107
    recognition programs and events, 119, 121
extension services, 62, 68, 131, 161, 163

F

501c3 status, 61, 85–87, 91, 93
fall cleanup, 120, 125, 166
Fall Creek Gardens Urban Growers Resource Center
    (Indianapolis, IN), 52
fall education topics, 164–167
fall sowing, 169, 170, 174, 181
fall volunteer event, 120–121
farm gardening. *See* row gardening
farmers as participants, 25, 27, 29
farmers' markets, 12, 30, 31
Feed Two Birds with One Worm (Santa Cruz, CA), 31
feedback, soliciting, 37, 121
fences
    in an area with busy streets, 23
    costs, 72–73
    as a design consideration, 76
    fence-free for access to produce, 28, 72
    municipal requirements, 63, 75
    to reduce theft, 63, 72, 75, 106
Filipowski, Joseph, 27
fire hydrants, 64–65
flowers that attract beneficial insects, 157
food, purpose of growing
    for community meals, 23, 31
    for distribution through CSAs, 31
    for food pantries, 22
    for individual or family use, 22, 23, 25–26, 27
    in mission development, 20
    for school lunch program, 30
    to sell to farmers' markets, 30, 31
food deserts, 20, 52, 93
food insecurity, 19, 27
FoodCorps, 30
fraternal organizations, 112
frost, 132, 165
fruit trees, 23
funding sources
    cash and in-kind donations, 93
    church-based, 25

considering in mission development, 20, 45
    grants, 29, 31, 86, 95
    groups that distribute funds, 91
    local banks, 98
    local donations, 21, 23, 25, 27, 29
    members, 21, 92
    organizations and corporate groups, 114
    produce sales, 31
    See also fundraising; sponsors and sponsorship;
        individual case studies, 21-33
fundraising
    crowd-sourced funding platforms, 92
    events, 29, 91–92
    role of boards in, 90
    volunteers with professional expertise in, 91, 111
fungal diseases, 152, 161, 162

G

garden amenities, 72
garden design
    choosing plants, 139
    consensus in, 77, 79, 81, 156
    design considerations, 76, 80–81
    planning during winter, 133
    removing complexity, 75
    visioning exercise, 78–79
garden location
    influence on mission and build, 20
    possibilities within the community, 59–63
    See also individual case studies, 21-33
garden name, 47
garden philosophy, 130
garden types, 66–67. *See also* allotment gardens; group
    production gardens
Garden Writers of America survey, 129
gardeners
    identifying experts, 81, 131
    and mission development, 20
    from outside groups, 28, 112–114
    See also volunteer management; volunteers;
        individual case studies, 21-33
garlic (*Allium sativum*), 174–175
gates, 80, 106
gazebos, 72
genetically engineered (GE) seeds, 142
genetically modified (GMO) seeds, 142
grant funding, 86
grant proposals, 95
graphic designers, 111
grassroots gardening movement, 10

green beans (*Phaseolus vulgaris*), 144, 148, 154, 175–176
green peppers. *See* peppers
greenhouses and hoop houses, 72, 148
greens, leafy, 134, 145, 147
grewbie gardeners, 131
grills, 72
ground cherries and tomatillos (*Physalis* sp.), 184–185
group decision-making. *See* consensus
group production gardens
    addressing soil quality, 68
    description, 67
    designing for light requirements, 76
    irrigation systems in, 64
Grow2Give (Chicago, IL), 22
Growing Together at the Gathering (Fargo, ND), 26
Growing Together Community Gardens (Fargo, ND), 25–26
growing zones, 132
growth habit, 144
Guadalupe Montessori School garden (Silver City, NM), 29–30

H

Habitat for Humanity, 31
handouts
    basic drawings of layout, 78
    hints for distribution during meetings, 43
    list of attributes of a successful group, 40
    as marketing/recruiting tools at events, 121, 123
    mission questionnaire, 47
hardiness, 132, 145, 165
harvesting
    in collective and allotment gardens, 112, 160
    "cut and come again" method, 147
    managing, 112, 160
    staggered plantings, 150
    See also individual plant profiles, 169-185
herbs
    in combo gardens, 67
    as perennials, 137
    that attract beneficial insects, 157
hold harmless waivers, 96, 105, 107, 108, 111, 112
Home Depot, 23
The Homeless Garden Project (Santa Cruz, CA), 31–33
hoop houses and greenhouses, 72, 148
hoses
    and backflow protectors, 65
    as basic supplies, 71

connections to fire hydrants, 64–65
handling in community gardens, 50, 64, 107
methods of use, 151–152
shutting off, 107
hospitals as partners, 54
hot peppers. *See* peppers
hot season crops, 145

I

Ibarra, George, 27
immigrant populations, 10, 36
indoor spaces, 23, 31
inground beds
    vs. raised, 66–67
    soil in, 62, 68
insects
    around compost, 70, 74
    attracting beneficial, 156–157
    and chemical pesticides, 141
    good and bad bugs, 156–159
    neighbor concerns, 70, 74
    See also pests
institutions as sources of land, 60
insurance
    directors and operators, 90
    liability, 89, 94, 96, 105
intensive gardening
    minimization of weeds, 163
    row planting/intensive gardening conversion table, 138
    square-foot gardening elements of, 137–138
Internet-based tools
    for collecting funds, 99
    for fundraising, 92
    garden planners, 133
    registration systems, 104, 105
Intuit GoPayment, 99
Ioby, 92
irrigation systems, 64, 65

J

jobs. *See* tasks

K

kale (*Brassica oleracea* var. *acephala*), 148, 176–177
Kickstarter, 92

L

land options, 60–63
landscape professionals, 69–70

laws and regulations
  bylaws, 90
  non-profits vs. for-profits, 86
  permits, 65, 72
  on remediating contaminated soil, 62
layout. *See* garden design
lead contamination, 62
leadership
  boards and board members, 87, 88–90
  characteristics of a good leader, 49–52
  vs. organizing, 18
  top-down and bottom up approaches, 18
leaf miners, 158
leafy greens, 134, 145
Lee, Paul, 33
legal professionals, 88, 94, 111
lettuce, 143, 147, 148
liability
  addressed in MOU agreements, 89
  hold harmless waivers, 96, 105, 107, 108, 111, 112
  insurance, 89, 94, 96, 105
  using legal professionals, 94, 96
listening, 51
lists of plants
  cool and hot season crops, 145
  crops for part and dappled sun, 134
  crops for staggered plantings, 150
  direct-seeded crops, 148
  by hardiness, 165
  perennials, 137
  sizes at full maturity, 136
  value/space comparisons, 135
lumber, 82
Lutheran Social Services, 25, 26

M

mandates
  conflicting, 63
  educational, 26, 33, 75
  mutually beneficial, 60, 112
  of outside volunteer groups, 112
  role in mission development, 20
  social, 52
  See also individual case studies, 21–33
Master Gardeners/expert gardeners
  to assist with pest problems, 161
  hands-on sessions taught by, 153
  identifying in the community, 81, 131
  including in events, 120, 122, 124
Meals on Wheels, 23

media permissions form, 96–97, 105
meetings
  as foundation, 35–36
  how-to instructions, 37
  agendas, 38–41
  introductory, 36
  first, 40–43
  second, 44–47
  third, 76–81
  bike racking of topics, 42, 43, 48
  reconvening and sharing foundational experiences, 167
  small-group breakouts, 41, 43, 48, 77–79
melons, 148, 154
membership fees, 92
Memorandum of Understanding (MOU), 87–89
MIAG Center for Diverse Women and Families (Ontario, Canada), 23
micro greens, 147
microclimate, 27
minority populations. *See* diversity and diverse populations
mission and mission statements
  as communication vehicle in fundraising, 91
  as consensus-driven, 19, 45, 47, 48
  developing, 19–20, 47
  importance of, 45
  influence on build, 20, 75
  word choice in, 47
  See also driving forces in garden genesis; *individual case studies,* 21-33
mission questionnaire, 20, 44, 47
mission-driven approaches. *See individual case studies,* 21-33
money management
  basics, 97–99
  budgets, 91, 97–98
  phasing of garden development, 81, 92
  researching costs, 81
  using accounting professionals, 111
MOU (Memorandum of Understanding), 87–89
mulch
  as organic antidote to diseases, 161, 162
  plant trimmings as, 166
  for specific plants, 174, 175, 176, 178, 181, 182, 183
  wood chips as, 70
municipal and county land options, 62–63
Music and Garden Experts Night, 124
Music and Master Gardener series, 120
mustard greens, 148

N

National Gardening Association, 29
neighborhoods
    developing suburban, 24
    economically challenged, 28
    ethnically diverse, 23, 24, 25–26
    food insecure, 27
    high-density urban, 22
    industrial, 28
    of new Americans, 25
    role in mission development, 20
    See also individual case studies, 21-33
neighbors, concerns and objections of, 74
New York City (NY) parks, 63
nightshade family, 180, 184
nonprofit status, 85–90. *See also* 501c3 status

O

OASIS (Indianapolis, IN), 52
odors, bad, 70, 74
okra (*Abelmoschus esculentus*), 136, 148, 177
OMRI (Organic Materials Review Institute), 141
onions (*Allium cepa*), 178
online aids. *See* Internet-based tools
organic gardening
    adhering to a group definition of, 66
    defined, 141
    as gardening approach, 106, 141
    importance of soil, 140–141
    pest and disease management, 140, 141, 156,
        158–159, 160–162
    seeds, 143
    and water backflow protectors, 65
    See also Peterson Garden Project
Organic Materials Review Institute (OMRI), 141

P

parks and park districts, 63, 71
parsley, 148
partners and partnerships
    with established organizations, 52–53, 60, 114
    good press as motivating, 63
    impact of mission on types, 20, 45
    including in events, 121
    with local retailers, 52, 54, 119
    reciprocity, 53–55
    sponsoring a workday, 110
paths, 70, 76
Paypal, 99
peas (*Pisum sativum*), 148, 178–179

peppers (*Capsicum annuum*), 134, 148, 159, 179–180
perennials, edible, 137
perfectionism, 130
performance stages, 72, 81, 120
pergolas, 45, 71, 72, 81, 114
permaculture, 28, 106
pests
    bad bugs, 156, 158–159
    healthy soil as resistant to, 140
    organic management of, 140, 141, 156, 158–159,
        160
    rats and vermin, 74
    See also plant diseases
Peterson Garden Project (Chicago, IL)
    communication with gardeners, 130
    educational mandate and build, 75
    educational programs, 117–118, 120, 131–132
    event stage, 120
    overview, 21–22
    partnerships, 61
    portability of, 75
    social programs, 120
    use of organic methods, 75, 141
    Volunteer of the Week program, 119
    watering techniques, 152
phasing of garden development, 81, 92
picnic tables, 72
plant diseases, 152, 160–162
plant lists. *See* lists of plants
planting, 145–150. *See also individual plant profiles*,
    169-185
plucots, 142
pole beans. *See* green beans
police as partners, 54
pollinators, 156
pollution, 62
potatoes (*Solanum tuberosum*), 180–181
powdery mildew, 161
private land options, 61–62
programs. *See* educational programs
public relations/marketing professionals, 111
Punjabi Community Health Services (Brampton,
    Ontario, Canada), 23

R

radishes (*Raphanus sativus*), 148, 181
rain barrels, 66
raised beds
    vs. inground in allotment gardens, 66–67
    materials and construction, 82–83
    in relation to fences, 76, 155

soil in, 62, 67, 140
    spacing plants in, 135, 138
    spatial understanding of, 136
rats, 74
refugee populations, 10, 25, 26
religious organizations
    intersection of mission with community gardens, 25,
        60
    as partners, 54
    as sources of land, 25, 60
    as sources of volunteers, 103, 112
    as sponsors, 23
respect, 50
retail businesses
    benefits of nearby gardens, 61
    as partners, 52, 54, 119
retirement centers as partners, 54
revenue sources. *See* funding sources
rhubarb, 137
root-bound plants, 150
row gardening, 137–138, 163
Rutgers University study, 10

S

safety practices
    establishing protocols, 82
    identifying and fixing problems, 96
    involving law enforcement agencies, 107
    providing drinking water, 108–109
    reporting concerns, 107
    with tools, 108
    when using fire hydrants, 64
Sahara Seniors Garden (Brampton, Ontario, Canada),
        23–24
salvaged materials, 28
school gardens, defined, 12. *See also* Guadalupe
        Montessori School garden
schools as partners, 54
SCORE, 87
seating, 71, 72, 80
security, 72–73
seed packages, 138, 143, 144
seed swaps, 118–119, 122–123
seedlings
    for first-year gardeners, 148
    vs. seeds, 148
    of specific vegetables, 149, 176, 178, 185
    transplanting methods, 149–150
seeds
    direct-seeded crops, 148

genetically engineered and modified, 142
    germination rates, 143, 148
    for leafy greens, 147
    lifespans, 143
    organic, 143
    saving, 142
    vs. seedlings, 148
    starting, 24, 148
    storing, 143
    swapping, 118–119, 122–123
seed-saving gardens, 67
seniors as gardeners, 64, 80, 83. *See also* Sahara
        Seniors Garden
septoria leaf spot, 162
service organizations, 91, 103, 112, 114
Service Technologies Corporation, 27
shared asset policies, 107
shelling peas. *See* peas
short-term gardens, 61, 69, 75
signage
    "*Enter at your own risk*," 97
    explaining public service aspects of garden, 73
    for finding meetings, 37
    orientation document as, 107
Sikh temple, 23
size of plants, 136, 144
small-group breakouts, 41, 43, 48, 77–79
snails and slugs, 159
snow peas. *See* peas
social mandates, 52
soil
    amending, 68, 140
    contamination of, 62
    crops that boost, 175
    depth for planting seeds, 145–147
    minimizing disturbances in, 140, 166
    in organic gardens, 140–141
    poor, 175
    in raised beds, 62, 67, 140
    sandy, 171
    temperature for germination, 145
    testing, 62, 68
South Asian heritage, 24
spacing plants
    planting schemes, 137–138
    in raised beds, 135, 138
    row planting/intensive gardening conversion table,
        138
    value/space comparisons, 135
    vine vs. bush varieties, 144
    See also individual plant profiles, 169-185

spinach (*Spinacia oleracea*), 148, 182
sponsors and sponsorship
    fiscal, 86–87, 93–94
    mission agreement with, 87, 93
    needs and goals of, 53
    role in mission development, 20
    See also individual case studies, 21-33
spring education topics, 139–152
spring events, 119
sprinklers, 152
Square, 99
square-foot gardening. *See* intensive gardening
squash. *See* summer squash
squash vine borer, 159
stages, event, 72, 81, 120
staggered planting, 150
stakes, 155, 159, 174, 179, 185
storage areas, 42, 71, 72, 80, 107
storing vegetables. *See individual plant profiles*, 169-185
straw as mulch, 173, 174
sugar snap peas. *See* peas
summer education topics, 153–163
summer events, 119–120
summer squash (*Cucurbita pepo*), 144, 148, 182–183
sun
    crops for part-and dappled, 134
    requirements as design factor, 76, 80
    when starting seeds, 148
sunflowers, 136, 157
support structures. *See* trellising
sustainability
    and effective organizing, 18
    funding for the future, 95
    indoor spaces for, 23
    of school gardens, 12
Swiss chard (*Beta vulgaris* subsp. *cicla*), 148, 183–184

T

tasks
    communal, 166
    maintenance chores, 106, 109, 110, 112, 160, 163
    meaningful work concept, 109
    non-gardening, 121
    short-term/one-time projects, 109
    See also specific tasks such as weeding, harvesting, etc.
tatsoi, 148
tax-exempt status. *See* 501c3 status
teachers
    displaced from an agricultural past, 36

finding and cultivating, 131
    as volunteers working with children, 26
    See also Master Gardeners/expert gardeners
thanking volunteers. *See* expressing appreciation
theft deterrence, 72–73, 75, 106
tomatillos and ground cherries (*Physalis* sp.), 184–185
tomato blight, 161
tomato hornworm, 159
tomatoes (*Lycopersicon esculentum*)
    germination rates, 148
    information on seed packages, 144
    need for full sun, 134
    plant profile, 185
    planting seedlings, 149
    'Sungold' and 'Better Boy' varieties, 142
    supporting, 155
toxic chemicals
    creosote, 82
    lead, 62
    least toxic, 160
trash, removing, 110, 112
trellising
    with cages, 155, 185
    on fences, 76
    role in pest and disease prevention, 156, 159
    of specific vegetables, 154–155, 173, 174, 175, 179, 185
    with stakes, 155, 159, 174, 179, 185
    structures from salvaged objects, 28
    varieties requiring physical support, 144
Tri-Neighborhood Community Garden (Norfolk, VA), 27–28
tubers, 180
turnips, 148

U

United Kingdom, hardiness data, 132
United States Department of Agriculture (USDA)
    hardiness zone map, 132
    hardiness zones, 145
    National Organic Program, 143
    organic standards, 141
untidiness, 75
urban agriculture as a term, 11
urban farms, defined, 11
Urban Patch (Indianapolis, IN), 52
USDA. *See* United States Department of Agriculture

V

varieties
    determinate and indeterminate, defined, 144

hybrid, 122, 142, 173
open-pollinated, 119, 122, 142
vegetable profiles, 169–185
vermin, 74
victory gardens, 20, 75, 129
vining varieties, 144
visioning exercises, 77–79
visitor policies, 106
volunteer management
consequences of non-participation, 106, 115
key elements for engaging volunteers, 103
organizing a skilled base, 111
orientation, 105, 106–107
recruiting, 109
registration, 104
service-learning hours, 108, 112, 114
spaces for, 105
workdays, 108, 110, 113
See also expressing appreciation
Volunteer of the Week program, 119
volunteers
with business skills, 110–111
mandatory hours, 106, 115
minors, 108
non-gardening, 110–111, 121
outside groups, 28, 112–114
personality types, 114
sources of, 103
See also volunteer management

W

water
for drinking, 108
standing, 74, 179
viable sources for, 63–66, 76

Water Ambassadors, 152
water backflow protectors, 65
watering
avoiding overhead methods, 152
in collective vs. allotment plots, 112
etiquette, 107
frequency and techniques, 151–152
orientation information for volunteers, 107
"water me" system, 152
See also hoses; individual plant profiles, 169-185
watering cans, 64, 71, 151
watermelon, 141
wecangrowit.org (blog), 130
weeding as garden task, 106, 109, 110, 112, 163
weeds
barriers in raised beds, 82
identifying, 163
intensive gardening and, 163
rules for unweeded plots, 106
wood chips to suppress, 70
winter programs, 118–119, 133–138
winter squash, 144, 148, 154
wood chips, 70–71
workdays, 108, 110, 113
workplace gardens, 11, 61
World War II victory gardens, 20, 75, 129

Y

yellow crookneck squash. See summer squash
youth centers as partners, 54

Z

zucchini. See summer squash

ABOUT THE AUTHOR

© Jen Moran

LaMANDA JOY is an award-winning Master Gardener and the founder and executive director of Peterson Garden Project, a gardening education program in Chicago, Illinois, that converts unused city land into large-scale community garden learning labs, teaching thousands of people to grow their own food. A nationally recognized expert, lecturer, and writer on urban edible gardening, she is the author (with Theresa Gale) of *Fearless Food Gardening in Chicagoland*, and creator of the acclaimed blog *The Yarden*. LaManda has also served on the board of directors of the American Community Gardening Association, is a recipient of the Illinois Governor's Sustainability Award, has been featured in the Mrs. Meyers Clean Day Grow Inspired film series, and was highlighted in the recent documentary *Food Patriots*. She has lectured on historical victory gardens at the Library of Congress, the Field Museum, the Seed Savers Exchange Annual Conference, and to other prestigious groups nationwide. She wants to teach everyone she meets to grow their own food. Seriously.

Illustrations by Scott Westgard, pages 80, 83, 134, 146, 147, 149, 151, 154, 155, 157.
All other illustrations ©Julia Sadler

Quotation from Michelle Obama, page 6, Whitehouse.gov (http://www.whitehouse.gov/
copyright)/CC BY 3.0 (http://creativecommons.org/licenses/by/3.0/us/)

The Haseltine Building
133 S.W. Second Avenue, Suite 450   6a Lonsdale Road
Portland, Oregon 97204-3527   London NW6 6RD
timberpress.com   timberpress.co.uk

Printed in The United States of America
Cover and text design by Laura Shaw Design, www.lshawdesign.com

Library of Congress Cataloging-in-Publication Data
Joy, LaManda.
  Start a community food garden: the essential handbook/LaManda Joy.—1st edition.
      pages cm
  Includes index.
  ISBN 978-1-60469-484-0
1. Community gardens. 2. Food crops. 3. Vegetables. I. Title.
  SB457.3.J69 2014
  635—dc23
                              2014020842

A catalog record for this book is also available from the British Library.